You Can't Be Serious

BOOKS BY MIKE PATERSON

With Love: Gifting Stories to Your Grandchildren

The Point at Issue: Petroleum Energy Politics in New Zealand, 1955–90

Goodstuff

Folk in Print: Scotland's Chapbook Heritage (with E.J. Cowan)

You Can't Be Serious

Mike Paterson

PHOTOGRAPHS BY MIKE PATERSON

Rock's Mills Press
Oakville, Ontario
2017

Published by
ROCK'S MILLS PRESS
www.rocksmillspress.com

Copyright © 2017 by Mike Paterson
PUBLISHED BY ARRANGEMENT WITH THE AUTHOR. ALL RIGHTS RESERVED.

Library and Archives Canada (LAC) Cataloguing in Publication data is available from the publisher. For this and other inquiries, contact us at customer.service@rocksmillspress.com.

DEDICATION

*To the wonderful women in my life:
my mother, Patricia;
my wife, Sue;
my daughter, Alannah
and my granddaughter, Amy*

Contents

	Introduction	1
1.	Origins	3
2.	Time: A Reflection	15
3.	Economics and the Artless Bystander	25
4.	Cultures of One	42
5.	Seeking Selfhood	55
6.	It's All Just Stories	67
7.	Wildernesses	81
8.	Religion	94
9.	Sources ... e.g., Christianity	106
10.	Why Not?	124
	References	141

Thank you

In addition to my loving family and my many dear, forbearing friends in New Zealand, Scotland, Canada and elsewhere, I'd like to thank my friends with the Agape Faith Kingdom Ministries' community at Sandys, Bermuda, for their welcome, encouragement and blessing ... particularly Anthony Steede, Lynn Landy, Kenneth Fox and fellow writer Karla Trott.

You Can't Be Serious

Introduction

THAT the world's not what it was should be no surprise. What is surprising is that human activities now enfold complexities that, even if we don't understand them, seem certain to decide the fate of every living organism. We need to know that the future's now our inescapable responsibility.

Not one cubic centimeter of the biosphere, atmosphere or ocean depths remains wholly untouched or unaffected by human interventions of one kind or another. Nuclear power, mass extinctions, the impacts of fertilizers, forestry, fossil fuels, and new materials: the evidence is indelibly laid down, even now, in the geological record. And, as each intervention has rippled through the whole, it's triggered unforeseen changes in places none of us have ever thought to look. Change begets more change, changes interact with each other and permeate things we never meant to mess with. And the tide's rising.

The old crusade to wrest control from nature's whim, one that's long preoccupied Western cultures, has reached its "Jerusalem." And, like all victories, the outcomes, intentional and coincidental, aren't quite what we hoped or expected.

IT'S a bit embarrassing really. Our bluffs, our boasts of unimpeachable intellect, are all being called into question.

Christian Schwägerl, author of *The Anthropocene: The Human Era and How It Shapes Our Planet*, told *New Scientist* writer Rowan Hooper that, rather than our long-established assumption that there's this "big, inexhaustible, alien space out there that we call *the environment*"—the source of our food and raw materials and the dumping ground for our waste—nature will become the *in-vironment*: "something we are deeply connected with."[1] A massive conceptual shift's called for, one based on partnership with nature rather than possession. It seizes us at personal, social and political levels.

So, what next?

"Don't get colonized by destructive industries," was Christian Schwåagerl's advice: "Enjoy breathing, eating, being in a forest or a green city space, enjoy helping others [and] paying attention to the colors and smells and creatures around you. In the Anthropocene we may one day cherish a square meter of wilderness as much as a painting of the same size by Van Gogh or Cézanne." Schwägerl's isn't a solitary voice. Nor is he the spokesman of global consensus. But he does grasp the breadth of reasoned anxiety.

This isn't to suggest that everyone has to see the "new Earth" the same way. Rather, the "new Epoch" imposes responsibilities on us all to measure our ways of living against the sorts of options that are still open to life—all life—on Earth.

Unsure of my own readiness for what lies ahead, I found myself sifting through my own experience, thinking, feelings and appreciations of life and was led to a "meaning of everything" that lies in uncertainty, in mystery and unknowables.

It came down to a choice far more complicated and difficult than it might seem: a choice between raw fear and unqualified trust. Fear, it seems to me, has botched hope for far too much of human history; unqualified trust has rarely been given a fair go. Trust in what? That's a good question. But I'd also want to ask "fear of what?"

My answer to both questions has to be: "I don't know."

I do know, though, that fear inhibits while trust liberates. And living in trust is not only more motivating and energizing than living in fear: it's heaps more fun. Curiosity takes me further when I trust.

Living in trust is a fair definition of "faith" and, in using that term, I don't mean the strangulation of intellect that's become a widely held stereotype of organized religion in the West. Nor do I mean sentimental soft-headedness.

So ... what follows is perusal of options. I hope you find encouragement here to embrace the Anthropocene with qualified joy. But joy nonetheless.

—Mike Paterson, Summer 2016

1 Origins

EAST COAST, NORTH OF GISBORNE, NEW ZEALAND

*Once I learned that
full engagement
with anything
on my own terms
was impossible ...
assurance, of a sort,
began to seep in.*

WHERE does it all begin?

Origins are elusive. There's conception and birth: I remember neither.

Nor do I find a "me" in the faded baby photographs my parents took on the lawn one sunny morning so many years ago. I have no recollection of learning to walk, or talk, or read. It's all a blank. My earliest memory is of a dog's big, wet, bright-pink tongue.

So, as people, where can we say we begin?

We grow a little and become individuals. Then, as individuals, we interact with others, start learning the first words of our native language and move into the anteroom of a culture. Imagination lights our play, and we're drawn into social interactions. Personality forms—a moment as amazing as birth—and with it, the origins of an identity: the day we realize we're alive, the day we become recognized participants in human society.

Or did the affectionate little mongrel my parents called Teddy lick me into being?

Life has lots to do with chemistry and energy. Fickle but purposeful, they get together and animate substances as unique, identifiable, active creatures for a time, then abandon them. But the side of life we're most immediately familiar with is consciousness: a peculiarly personal phenomenon poised like a bridge between life and matter.

Standing on the bridge, there was a time when I thought it was my bridge, and that I stood there aloof and alone as if others had not shaped me by being the stuff of my experience and the mediators of my "self" expression. I'd extricated myself from the rough clamor of childhood with a firm conviction that I existed as a unique, independent, autonomous being, charting my own, deliberate course through the press of humanity. I'd been persuaded that existential chasms divide *people* and *animals* and, just as deeply, separate *these* people from *those* people: *me* from *you*, and *us* from *them*.

Like others of my time and place, and with their complicity, I came to a clear idea of myself existing in a society at struggle, a society that told stories of implacable rivalry—person with person, and person with life at large: pathways of conflict and power. This is the derangement of Hollywood's lonesome, cowboy-hero fantasy: it fed a gnawing fear that somebody might actually call my bluff—that I wasn't as socially adept as my fabricated "image" might suggest, or as quick on the draw.

> *ODD, isn't it? That, after thousands of years, we still cling to constantly contradicted illusions of permanence, uniqueness and fixedness. Posterity, stability, certainty, straight-line projections: they all take immense effort. And, like the stability of a gyroscope or a toy top, they are sustained by the velocity of our senselessly spinning souls.*

FALLING in puppy-love gave me my first glimpses of life's tide dashing the sandcastles of my selfhood. Love demands transparency. My impulse, of course, was to resist. I was young and vain. But to resist vulnerability is to close to love.

Love's too broad and ample a force to be wholly swallowed up by just one other person. Accepted, its energies rise. They overflow to reach every shore, calling lovers back to realizations of their humanity. And loving-vulnerability illumines goodness all the way to the ends of the Earth.

So I find myself, my real, flawed, love-unworthy self, called back to life: catapulted over the hurdles, tumbled into the gaps: a swerving and headlong dash. And, while the world so urgently plunges me into beauty after beauty, mystery within mystery, from fright into fright and joy upon joy. Where's the need for questions?

What was the question?

Yes: where did we begin?

> *In the beginning that was so long ago, a straight thing, an arrow perhaps, was launched into the chaos, unity parted and became myriad; elements became substance, and substance made form possible. We are form trying to remember unity; straightness trying to remember the path before there were paths, shamed to be mere fragments. We are babes awakening, we are storms gathering, we are waterfalls tumbling, we are geese taking wing to escape the gathering chill. We are incomplete. We are in motion. Knowing that brokenness can be mended impels us to fly, even if we are unbroken, because we know all things break in the end. So the energies of life lead us away to seek the edges of our being.*

WE'RE suckers for a story. The old nature-nurture debate sidesteps what I'd declare to be humanity's most decisive formative force: narrative. Narratives—stories—are what we need to satisfy our cravings for meaning.

> *In the beginning was the Word ...*

SO it is that every culture seems possessed by some sort of a creation story—though *foundation story* might be a better term. Never mind: what's needed is a story that puts the earth beneath its hearer's feet.

At school in New Zealand, we had to memorize the succession of British monarchs. Expecting barefoot, beach-happy, footy-playing primary school kids in a multicultural classroom in the Southern Hemisphere to commit this list of names to memory as their foundation story—from Ethelred to Elizabeth—still seems surrealistically absurd to me.

> *... and the word was "god."*

A PARTICULAR gift of my youthful intimacy with the ocean was experience of my own vulnerability, made clear in the mirror held up to me by a strange, bewitchingly beautiful world.

IT begins in the sea, like time: the long, regular oceanic risings and valleyings, the sea's sharper breaking, pitching and heaving, its rush to shores and hissing retreats, and, beneath the sinewy flow of currents, a dark, seeming stillness. And beneath even that, there continue the achingly slow journeying of the Earth's mantle itself, inexorably sliding and folding under to soften and grow molten or, prised upwards, rising and hardening so that the seas toss their wrack against new shores while still gnawing patiently away at the old.

It all begins with the sea, like the lurch of a surfboard catching the wave, the heaving, changing otherness of it, the smell of it, the taste of it, the ever-presence of it; the plunge and crackle of surf, the yawing roll of deep ocean swells, transparent black under a keel, and the trailing wake that ever-so-slowly vanishes; oyster-clad rocks and spray-drenched mussel beds, tresses of kelp reaching from the rocks, the thud and thrust of a filling sail and a ship's churning wallow through the waves, that ship-smell of tar and cordage and iodine, the glowing trails of fish through luminescent subtropical water at night while overhead the stars reflect on the open water where swells rise and fall as they did for millions of human lifetimes before the first human appeared, eons of motion, never the same, never different.

You can see the dorsal fins of basking sharks and sunfish. Their forms, far more ancient than ours, sing of primality—where the sun bakes down and the wind is low, the surface-parting puffs and inhalations of whales rising from their ringing depths, the majestic passage of sharks, the other-worldliness of diving deep where color is washed away and countless creatures live out lives that shake off all that we can learn from our circumscribed lives on Earth to inhabit a three-dimensional freedom that surpasses even that of the globe-circling albatross. The loneliness of the sea's constant, animated companionship, its power to console or destroy: this is where it all begins.

ONE of my favourite foundation stories has long been that of the minority Ainu culture of Japan. It tells of a tireless little bird, a wagtail, that flits over a vast primeval bog, flicking water to this side and to that, revealing the earth that it gradually but finally flattens to firmness: a task that takes a near eternity.

Then there's an intriguing ancient Egyptian image of humankind having arisen from the tears of the creator god.

MORE recently, biologists Nick Lane and Bill Martin gave me another tale.[2] In this story, there was a particular moment on a particular day—about two billion years ago—when an archaeon engulfed a bacterium. Both are microscopic, single-celled entities with no cell nucleus: two dumb but distinctively different little proto-organisms that were among the first living stuff on the planet.

The little bacterium survived inside the archaeon as a kind of biological power-pack: the first mitochondrion. The result was a new kind of creature with enough vigour to start hatching new gene arrangements, and multi-celled descendants, eukaryotes, like us.

Before that, all life was locked up in single cells.

That one wee bacterium fuelled the future of life on Earth. Its memorial is found in the DNA that's engraved in every mitochondrion of our body's every living cell.

The extraordinary detail is that the pairing happened just that once. We know, because a second pairing would carry a separate genetic signature. But there's just the one, despite archaeons and bacteria having flourished on the Earth for a billion years previously, being with us still and being extraordinarily prolific. Scientists tell us that a gram of soil can contain 100 million of them, representing as many as a million different species. They teem in the oceans too, and in our intestines where, without them, we couldn't digest food. Higher life was a bizarrely improbable event.

The new creature's descendants grew, and found that sex could be fun: the whole genetic diversification and natural selection thing kicked in. And life on Earth began blazing away like skyrockets from a fireworks' factory fire: plants and animals in all of their startling diversity were hurled into being.

And us?

We're eukaryotes too. Every living thing is related and every living thing more complicated than a bacterium can trace its origins to that special, singular day when the archaeon got together with the bacterium. There is no "us" and no "them." We ought to get together with our kin and celebrate an annual Global Eukaryote Day: a universal festival of feasting, a celebration of sexuality, diversity, life's elemental unity, life's possibilities, mysteries and connectedness—of the marvellous beauty of all living things and our capacities to experience them: a festival of consciousness, emotion, perception and the beauty of life from amoebae to apple trees and redwood pines, angelfish and us, and including clams, cows, sloths, scorpions, birds, turtles, guinea pigs, snakes, toads, beetles and butterflies, dogs and cats ... and all of the plants and animals we don't know about yet because we're still discovering the bounty of our planet. Nature's a kaleidoscope, a great, beautiful kaleidoscope and we're in the midst of it. So it's way past time to give thanks to the bacterium and archaeon.

But this is where science lets us down, and lets itself down: ritual and celebration.

The word was with god ...

IT was the Enlightenment that forced us to our knees before the idols as well as the essence of reason. Reason's reward has been raw, enormous, forceful power.

It swept aside the Old World autocrats who boarded history's tumbrils apparently unaware that the "divine right" by which they'd ruled had been nothing more than a cruelly imposed charade. Reason was irreconcilable with their conceptions of "god."

Sharing this kingly view (that "god" and "reason" stand in necessary opposition to each other) reasonable men—and they really were mostly men—concluded that their reasonability crowned them the new custodians of truth. It was a dynastic as well as a moral and philosophical coup.

Reason was licenced to root out superstition wherever it lingered. The old-fashioned exploitative imperialism that stuffed kings' coffers became modern, appropriative progress that enriched the plutocrats of reason.

Mystery—the gods' elixir of life—could survive only behind the curtains of time ... so they set about parting the drapery. Behind one set of curtains they found the lingering shadow of an inexplicable singularity that flew apart in the Big Bang. Behind the other, they saw only the implacable darkness of an ever-expanding Universe reaching far beyond the inevitable demise of our particular little sun. Eternity and infinity remain hypotheses and God is nowhere to be seen. What, apart from ultimate oblivion in the expanding Universe, could possibly transcend human reason?

We owe our gloom about all of this to some mistaken ideas about rationality, reason and our self-evaluated intelligence as a species. Mystery can strike us as personal failure, as an embarrassment. How often, just for example, when we've done something on a whim, do we feel an immediate impulse to come up with a "good reason" for it?

Take breakfast. Here's a reflection on reasoning from a 2013 Kellogg's press release announcing the U.S. launch of its first hot cereal:

> *When considering a nutritious breakfast, 54 per cent of consumers think fiber is important and 49 per cent think protein is important. Special K Nourish hot cereal features a unique whole grain blend, including quinoa, oats, barley and wheat, and each serving provides 8 grams of protein and 5 grams of fiber. This is the first-ever hot cereal from Special K in the U.S. and it debuts in three flavors: maple brown sugar crunch, cranberry almond, and cinnamon raisin pecan.... Nuts and fruit are provided in a removable cap and can be stirred into the hot cereal for a delicious taste experience.*[3]

SERIOUSLY ... what did you eat, or not eat, for breakfast this morning? And why? Really?

Rather than admit that we simply "felt like it," we might feel oddly obliged to make up something. We fabricate. Our "reasons" can start persuading even us. They can bully us into denying our intuition and impetuosity, even when we've just acted on them. They deny us opportunities to better understand ourselves.

It's too bad. It makes us less likeable.

CONTEXTS play a big part in shaping the way we think.

Knowing this, architects create spaces that welcome us or impose upon us, inhibit us or excite us. It's not to cultivate musical appreciation that retailers pipe music into their stores; it's because research has shown that it increases sales. Lighting, colours, store layout, smells, loyalty cards, staff dress codes and customer interactions ... it's all been studied.

As our homes swell with memories, they can bring us joy or despond. Sounds, colours, forms, smells—things we can often take charge of quite easily—can manage our mood. Redecorating, or not, is our response.

Places exercise our emotions. And familiarity can deepen attachment, or alienation. Think of how your emotions and expectations are governed by time spent in the waiting room of, say, a doctor, a lawyer, a tax consultant, a gym, a mall, or the triage room at a hospital. It's unusual not to play the part that's expected of us.

One of the excitements of travel is the limbering up of our self-awareness, whether it's the debauch of a hen or stag party in Ibiza, the release of a mountainscape, the bustle of old, inner-city Naples, or the awe that the simplicity of somewhere like Iona can inspire.

Tourism sets out to modulate these experiences, and turn a profit from softening the shocks, amplifying the highs and optimizing tourists' opportunities to spend. Sometimes it overwhelms them. A gondola ride in Venice can be as romantic as a traffic jam; St. Peter's Basilica can be as edifying as an inner-city railway station at rush hour. Seen cruelly and critically, the souvenirs on offer in such places typically parody local culture, insult the intelligence of those who buy them and mock the aesthetic capacities of both. But they work because—a bit like family heirlooms—they help us to recharge otherwise fading recollections of what we imagined in that place, at that time. They're personal mementos. They work uniquely for us, and they'll probably still be around after the next garage sale.

ANYWAY, our popular notions of where factuality and hard-headedness fit into all of this are not necessarily less erratic than our whimsy and nostalgia. And, we should allow, whimsy and nostalgia are valid emotions.

You'll hear educated, science-respecting people assert, for example, that we use only 10 per cent of our brains, that the Earth's shadow shapes the phases of the Moon, that we should all drink eight glasses of water a day, that humans existed on Earth before the last dinosaurs fell extinct, that population growth is accelerating, that there's zero gravity in space, that hair and fingernails keep growing after you die, that there are non-surgical ways to make a penis bigger, that it's good to splash hydrogen peroxide onto wounds as a disinfectant, that the colour red provokes bulls to attack, that there's a cure for split ends, that not winning a lottery betters the odds of winning the next time—and that science is bound to come running and mop up after our every social, moral and environmental blunder, even climate change, without upsetting our economy or precious lifestyle.

The actual impacts of science on human experiences of life, community and society go largely unquestioned and scientists, reasonably, tend to deny responsibility for the abuses their work facilitates. Most of us are unaware of scientific progress until some surprising new product captivates our attention.

And, even in addressing our deepest anxieties, the most idealistic science can find it impossible to please everyone. Death, for example—the one experience we'll all share—terrifies many. So medical science has found ways, at a price, to postpone death. Hugely. A few people, going further than sound science, invest heavily in having their corpses deep-frozen, hoping they'll one day be restored to conscious life for purposes other than invasive research. At the same time, back in the real world, we're hearing calls to enshrine a right to die and the legalization of assisted suicide because life can become unendurable. Meanwhile, it's well known that the surest way to die young is to endure poverty. It could be a conflicting experience to posthumously discover that being dead is a great way to exist.

That's the thing, isn't it? Not knowing bothers us. But knowing—in almost any direction we look— is a challenge beyond us.

And the things that become most familiar to us? They can trip up our expectations too. Television, hailed as a breakthrough educational tool, has flourished by promoting functional addiction to progressively more vacuous entertainment and celebrity, a role that other media are now usurping. Computing, hailed as the herald of a greatly shortened working hours, has, at least in North America, widely seen them extended. Yet, with robotics and artificial intelligence, the number of jobs is expected to contract, dramatically. Will we still stigmatize the jobless[4] when the jobs have gone?

And so it goes....

THE trouble seems to be that behind every experience, image or event, there's a deeper story. And, beneath that, yet another, even deeper.

And could it be that our thinking is confined by our humanity? We have boundaries defined by what we need for simple survival: we have boundaries when it comes to survivable temperatures, oxygen levels, nutriment intakes. Surrounded as we are by specifically human horizons like these, isn't it a sure bet that we also have intellectual and psychological limits?

Does our physical existence not lock us within a closed system? The universe we know of and experience is all held within the extent and capacities of our imagination, a realm of uniquely human consciousness. It feels like a very big realm from our point of view, even before clever technology stretches the boundaries, but I'm not sure we can claim to transcend the traps of tautology, of seeing things as true because that's the way we experience and are able to describe them—while greater, over-arching realities perch out of reach.

Mathematics jets us over a few rainbows, to places that add scope to our technological creativity while, at the same time, defying explanation. They're logical phantoms: they work, but in ways that disturb even the mathematicians' sense of what's real. In their own ways, our arts, rituals and other intense emotional experiences can give us similar jolts of inexplicable realization. But, wherever we go, we remain mere human beings, mirroring each other's limitations and possibilities.

A QUESTION can ring-fence the answer. But a stupid question can generate as much data as a good one. That can be a problem.

In science, stupid questions are usually short-lived. Phrenology is a scientific embarrassment that comes to mind. Worse dangers spring from clumsy attempts by news media to explain increasingly complicated scientific findings to people who have all sorts of other things on their mind. This helps stupid questions to muddy a lot of water while they're around.

But there's something we should ponder these days: most research has long been applied. This means that a lot of attention is paid to particular questions posed by deep-pocketed corporate and military funders. The answers are bound to favor the funders' interests, which may—or may not—coincide with humanity's needs or interests.

Something science has often been ill-equipped to do has been to convincingly upset our values, principles and priorities, rather than serving them. And that's our fault. We are dead set against bad news. Back in 1988, for example, I reviewed a coffee table book for the *New Zealand Herald*. *The Home Planet* published 150 breathtaking full-color photographs of Earth taken from space. The first two paragraphs of my review read: "Such *matters of fact* as the greenhouse effect, the hole in the ozone layer, acid rain and ground and water pollution are causing our global ecosystem to buckle at the knees. The blame can be laid only on the spectacular over-consumption of resources by a minority of the world's population." Indeed, concerns about coal's atmospheric impacts have been around since the early-to-mid-nineteenth century.

In 2015, 27 years later, with awareness of the Anthropocene shift, the problems became clearer but there was still a reluctance to put the planet and human survival ahead of short-term profit-taking.

> *WE have changed the atmosphere and thus we are changing the weather. By changing the weather, we make every spot on Earth man-made and artificial. We have deprived nature of its independence, and this is fatal to its meaning. Nature's independence is its meaning—without it there is nothing but us.*[5]

THE simple reality is that science generally amplifies the consequences of human impulses. It is, after all, a cultural creation.

In the contexts of its time and society, science is always moving on, widening and migrating from one conceptual geography to another, applying one paradigm and the next.

IT would be nice if we could all learn from that. But it's not that simple: science is often misunderstood as a search for certainties when it is, more crucially, the pursuit of questions.

The story of science, beneath the formal rigour of its language, is a necessarily human one. René Descartes, the fifteenth-century French military man whose mathematical genius paved the way for modern science, diaried that, in a series of three visions on the same night, the Angel of Truth revealed to him the secret connection between geometry and algebra. Then there's the story of the great Danish physicist, Niels Bohr, co-founder of quantum mechanics, who was asked by a student about the superstition attached to a horseshoe he'd nailed to the door of his summerhouse. Bohr denied believing that the horse shoe brought him luck, then mischievously added: "But I understand that it works whether you believe it or not."

Albert Einstein said his life work in physics was an extended meditation on a dream he'd had as a child: it was night, he was on a toboggan and the stars changed colour as the toboggan accelerated down the hill. And, in his late sixties, he described a moment he vividly remembered from his childhood: "I experienced a miracle ... as a child of four or five when my father showed me a compass." It excited him so much that he trembled and grew cold. "There had to be something behind objects that lay deeply hidden ... the development of (our) world of thought is in a certain sense a flight away from the miraculous."

Then there was 1969 Nobel-Prize-winning physicist Murray Gell-Mann's teasing quip that "if I have seen further than others, it is because I am surrounded by dwarfs." It was a playful barb that tweaked Charles Darwin's echoing of an old Roman acknowledgement about having stood "on the shoulders of giants."

SCIENTISTS are people too.

And what began as human engagement with immediate necessities now reaches deep into the Universe. The Universe remains a conundrum, or science would no longer be a career path.

A great part of science's energy is drawn from and inspires awe. It's an emotion that's not far from that which, for millennia, has been inspiring the religious and wisdom-seeking mystics of many cultures.

Science is firstly a witness and stimulus to human curiosity. It's our curiosity — our questions, not our answers — that makes us admirable. Science is a creative, exciting, enabling and imagination-fuelling expression of that curiosity. It serves us best when it nurtures our best impulses: to compassion, to delight, to possibility, to new sensations of existence, to deeper appreciation. It's a powerful tool and we are wonderful toolmakers.

But it's not the theory, technology or the mathematical formulae that *experience* mystery, awe, satisfaction and wonder. It's the human heart, mind and soul.

IT's our preconceptions that hold us back. Even before we reach their boundaries, they nag us to declare that we've reached the dangerous edge of reality.

It's these same preconceptions that hold our view of the world together: of course we're reluctant to let them go. They define us and, without them, our very sense of selfhood slips its moorings.

> *The Earth's axis of spin is tilted 23.5 degrees from its orbital plane around the sun. In its summer, one hemisphere tilts sunwards; in its winter, it inclines towards the outer edge of our solar system. Days shorten and lengthen; seasons come and go, and come again. Each night, the starry sky looks a little different.*
>
> > *... our planet is gently rocked from one season to the next.*
>
> *We're flying around the Sun at a speed of about 107,200 kilometers an hour. Meanwhile, travelling at about 220 kilometers a second, our Solar System is orbiting the centre of the Milky Way Galaxy once every 225 to 250 million years. (The Sun is thought to have made between 18 and 20 galactic orbits during its lifetime.)*
>
> > *... yet any one of us can watch a tree dance, hear a bird call, touch a warm smooth stone, smell an animal's presence or love-food cooking ... and experience the expansion of our being more readily than we can sense the extraordinary expansion of the "whole" that cradles us.*
>
> *At the same time, the Milky Way Galaxy is speeding away from all other visible galaxies as the expansion of the universe continues to accelerate:*
>
> > *... we are on a journey of significance, sustained by rhythms and immensities that reach far beyond our imaginations; we are "newness" in a generative and irresistibly dynamic universe.*

How good is it to be empowered by gratitude and joy to turn such vast and fleeting things into vibrancies of love?

SO, in the end, life has to rest on foundations of trust. Trust lets us experience existence beyond our safe preconceptions, as a way to approach the big, overarching mystery which begins within us, gives life its significance and, when we need it most, can root us in joy. There's a word for that kind of necessary trust: faith.

WHAT was the question?

Yes: where did we begin? Where do any of us begin? Perhaps every moment is a kind of beginning? Perhaps it's the most important?

The crow exults in morning gold;
the wind sings soft deliverance.
I blink at the new day into which
our Earth has turned, where buds
stare boldly at the rising heights
that lift the blush from naked dawn.
Despite my many cloaks,
I am a part of all this rude euphoria.

2
Time: A Reflection

HEALEY FALLS, ONTARIO

LYING in an influenza-induced miasma of misery, I had in my line of sight the face of a cheap, battery-powered alarm clock I'd bought at Boots on Sauchiehall Street in Glasgow for £5.

It was a square-faced, plastic-cased analog clock made in China with Arabic numerals, 1 through 12, and a second hand that made 60 sudden steps forward each minute, none of them quite aligning with the marks on the face. Every hour, it made 360 of these nervous little bunny-hops, degree by degree, around the circle. And, degree by degree, I drifted with it.

I dreamed of sailing, of my times at sea, and the activities of waiting and navigation that are a part of that. The geographic degrees, to which my toying thoughts wandered, each comprise 60 minutes—each a nautical mile. So I'd wooze away and half-dream about ships' wakes, heeling yachts and starry skies and the alluring smell of the sea. It seemed to relieve the congestion. Then I'd wake again in the same bed, in the same place, as though time made no difference at all. It was a "you-haven't-missed-a-thing" kind of clock.

Analog clocks like that pointedly describe a centre. Closer to that slowly revolving arbor at the centre, the hands travel more slowly than they do at their tips, where they nudge past the numbers. And it's the clock's tiny hub—its centre—that's pinpointed. It's a truthful way of representing time. Time is a local phenomenon. And the centre's a slow place.

"Time flies," we often hear, "when you're having fun." It's an airborne quality: *tempus fugit*—"time flies"—has for centuries been routinely stamped, engraved and cast on the faces of sundials and clocks. The image of winged time seems to have originated in the words of the Augustan era Roman poet Virgil: *fugit inreparabile tempus*: "time's flying by," in Peter Fallon's 2006 translation, "time we'll never know again."[6] Virgil was praising the virtues of the farmer's earthy life of focused hard work. In that context, Virgil's words confronted sloth, self-indulgence and distraction with a death mask.

EVERYDAY time is a culturally loaded values system. In mainstream Western society, we tend to divide time roughly into work and leisure. Both have fuzzy edges but, for adults, work and leisure often designate flows of money—in or out—and, like Virgil, separate productivity from self-indulgence and earning from spending. The ways we "use" or "spend" our time are as indicative of who we are and what we esteem as the ways we apply any other resource. And it's usually highly visible, helping to define our place and character in a community.

A relatively new value that's wormed its way into segments of Western society is the idea that work has a value for its own sake. It's an extension of Max Weber's idea of the Protestant work ethic that harnessed the will to work to the Protestant virtues of productivity and frugality. To grant ethical discernment to a hired employee would be a step too far in the mills of enterprise.

"TIME is money," some would have us believe. It's certainly a notion that handily holds a lot of us in thrall. I'm thinking of a man I met recently who held three jobs, one of which paid for childcare so he could work the other two. He was proud of his efforts, though he thought he was doing well when he got more than eight consecutive hours at home with his partner and their three children. They live on cheap food, wear secondhand clothing and have no "spare cash" for kids' sports, cellphones or day trips. They do have television.

The reality is that too many hard, dull, dirty, dead-end and part-time jobs reward one's time with poverty-level incomes. The stresses on families and the impacts on parenting, health, and social morale—the exclusion they inflict—are proof of exploitation and injustice. Work's rewards have to include the time, room and means for a fair family life. That's pretty much the baseline of sustainability and, until that baseline's met, society's failing and the economy is a sham.[7]

FEW primal cultures have felt as compelled as we do to be governed by the niceties of time. To traditionally-minded Inuit, for example, time is unapologetically subjective. Things happen when they happen, as they happen. The Inuit notion of time is "founded on the belief that one cannot, and ought not, assume that one has control over the world around one—whether at a physical or a metaphysical level," wrote researcher Nicole Gombay.[8] The Amondawa people of Brazil, on the other hand, find "time" in the types of work the seasons dictate, the daily passage of the sun and the shifting of social realities. A new child takes the name of his or her older sibling who, in turn like a new season, takes a new name.

It's time's markers, and the psychology of time, that vary from one culture to another.

And, while time is ours to shape, it's non-renewable. There are no top-ups. Virgil's death mask confronts us all. Each moment of life is unique and not one of them can be re-visited. Rather, thanks to our memories, those moments have played their part in molding us in our own particular way. We can let the time we're given drift by, or we can shorten it (which is effectively the same thing). We can spend it like a sailor, or nibble at it like a miser. We can "let go" of the past or agonize over it. But we cannot "un-live" it.

> *Time "hath, my lord, a wallet at his back, wherein he puts alms for oblivion," my dad used to say as a witticism when we were running late for some event or appointment. I think I knew quite young that the words were Shakespeare's but nothing about their context. I don't know that my dad did either, but he enjoyed the poetry and saw truth in the idea of "alms for oblivion" that he'd use to name urgencies of others' making. The quote is from* Troilus and Cressida; *the words come from the mouth of Ulysses. To my dad, they were about life's ephemerality, something he'd witnessed up close and first-hand as an infantry officer in Italy during the Second World War. There was no understanding fate's fickleness or justice when it came to life or death on the battlefield. Time was tossed in the air like dice. It rained down where it may.*

LIKE sound, smell, taste, touch and sight, time is one of our innate senses. But, lacking obvious receptors, it hasn't made the usual list of five. Nor did it even get ranked sixth: that went to the picking up of uncanny intuitions. Nonetheless, our bodies have built-in ways of tracking time's passage, and our light-sensitive circadian rhythms—managed by a nerve bundle in the hypothalamus called the suprachiasmatic nucleus—remind us to sleep and to waken. Generally, we perk up in the late morning, mid-afternoon and early evening.

Psychologists tell us that the "present"—the core of ongoing experience—seems to last for two-and-a-half to three seconds. It's a period of awareness that flutters between an unreliably remembered past and an unforeseeable future. Images and sensations flood in from our different senses, a bit like movie frames, to be smoothed and connected to sustain the impression of a meaningful flow. Memories help to give it direction. And, if things get too dramatic or busy, our physiology packs the extra inputs into our awareness by stretching time around them. We feel time slow down. Or stand still. Time seems to put elastic bindings around the inputs of our other senses. Meanwhile, our immediate experience is seeping through into long-term memory. This is a selective process, a sifting, that shapes the story we tell our friends afterwards. As time goes by, we often tweak these narratives here and there, and they come out just a little differently.

So time's bound up with our capacities to remember. And, just as our other senses can fool us with illusions and ambiguities, illusions and ambiguities of time and memory can mess with our awareness, impressions and emotions. It tantalises us with indescribable ideas like eternity, and flies by faster than our thoughts. We can measure time in nanoseconds, hours, decades, centuries, millennia and epochs, in seasons, in phases of the moon and by the height of the sun. We count its passing in ages, dynasties and eras. Each of its measures has its own limits, suited to some narratives and reflections more than to others.

With no sense of time at all, we'd be unable to experience rhythm or ride bicycles. We'd have no narratives and no gods. But, despite the part it plays in our lives, time is still one of the less understood aspects of human psychology.

> *Imagine time experienced by a band of hunter-gathers: a syncopation of incidents and occurrences that are stretched by memory across a regular, foreshortened background rhythm of days and nights. Think of temperate-climate farmers, attuned to seasons, and the seasonally changing length of days, punctuated by the repetitive, familiarized routines and tasks of cultivation, harvest and storage; skills and roles merging inseparably into identity. Or industrial workers, governed less by seasons than by employers' schedules and fiscal years, clocks, shifts and breaks, relieved by occasional holidays. Imagine time's passage for the computer-bound office worker: in constant light, temperature, sound and humidity levels, a hum interrupted by irregular meetings or breaks. And then there's the foraging for irregular, minimum wage work, paid by the hour, the insecurity and needful anxieties that characterize the experience of today's modern urban poor, barred from specialization by uncertainty and the notionally "unskilled" nature of their work. Each hour, then, is counted like a breath. Remember when time has seemed variously to crawl, to stop, or to bound by ... and those friends whose time seems always to be just out of step with yours, while others seem almost perfectly synchronized.*

ALBERT Einstein's theory of general relativity merged time with space as a unified entity called space-time that—bent by matter or energy—keeps our feet on the ground: the force of gravity. Quantum theorists see time, rather, as a universal background against which wave functions of probability batter themselves into realisation. All of this gets very difficult to visualize, and time, in this grand sense, is a mystery. Even the scientific definition of one second of time—a measure that's needed to pinpoint sequences and change in nature and experimentation—lies beyond any ordinary person's powers of visualization and estimation. It's based on the transition periods of the ground state of the cesium 133 atom at rest at absolute zero: 9,192, 631,770 of them.

"It is highly likely that what we think of as time emerges from some deeper, more primitive non-temporal structure," Dean Rickles, co-director of the Centre for Time at the University of Sydney, Australia, told a *New Scientist* writer in what was widely understood to have been 2011 (but which also was 4709 according to the Chinese calendar, a year of the rabbit; or 1432 in the Muslim calendar; and 1461 in the Armenian calendar ... or various other years in other calendars).

Meanwhile, the nature of Dean Rickles' "deeper, more primitive non-temporal" structure depends on a yet-to-be formulated theory of everything. That means "there is a long way to go," he said, "but it certainly seems that the concept of time will play a crucial role."9

> Like playful bears, the time-stuffed shuffling
> monsters that are our memories
> lead us on in their sniffing, foraging
> fanciful way;
> like water ... from melting ice
> their footfall makes the days translucent
> so colours, and the shapes of colours, run
> more real than the sticky, clinging stuff,
> the cloying gallimaufry that binds us,
> unseen and underfoot,
> and weighs down our clodded way,
> with all that we can never know.

SO, for now and for all practical purposes, time's local. And our analog clocks with their rotating hour and minute hands put time wherever they are put. There, they become the disseminators of time. Whether or not they're a few minutes "fast" or "slow" rarely matters: it's told time that we'll use as an organizing principle.

In one of its strongest forms, it's there in the sounding of bells and sirens, ordering unison and action. I'm thinking of the bells that governed our lives at boarding school and the ship's bells that passed responsibilities from one watch to the next in the Navy. For centuries, church bells synchronized the lives of European villagers. Their peals co-ordinated the components of community and the lives of neighbors, one with another.

At a more personal level, we set alarm clocks.

AH ... but I remember a wonderful clock from my childhood.

It was an old clock, a venerable clock: a "sit-down-and-unwind" kind of clock. It overflowed with time and shared it around the room. Time drifted from its tall oaken case, like morning mist. It ticked and it tocked, and it had to be wound by shifting weighted chains, a ritual I was always "too young" to perform. A long pendulum with a great brass weight swung sedately to and fro, and hid some inner mechanical sound that seemed from time to time to say "hush." It had twelve positions around its face too, but they were Roman numerals, and the "four" was "IIII" rather than "IV." It had no second hand. Every minute, the longer hand would quiver as some hidden, whirring, grinding took place, then sedately clunk forward.

Most wonderful of all were the chimes. Every quarter-hour, something would whirr and the chimes—as gently enchanting as cocoa and firelight—would slowly sound. All of this seemed so much more circumspect and less urgent, more malleable and relationship favoring, than sweep second hands and barefaced Arabic numerals. Without a second hand, time was freed to dawdle.

There was a lot of time for a lot of things back then. I had to practice the piano for half an hour when I got home from school, usually by way of the beach ... while the big hand went from the "VI" of half past five to the "XII" of six. Then I'd feed our dog, and wash and dress tidily for dinner at the "VI" of six-thirty. There was nothing much else to measure time by except the shifting light and "feel" of things in those media-free days. I remember wanting the clock's hands to sometimes move more quickly, sometimes more slowly: thirty minutes to get ready for dinner often left me twenty minutes to read books from the dining room bookcase. They got me interested in history before I heard of it as a subject at school.

That old clock, brought with my dad's family from Scotland, was passed on elsewhere when we moved to a new place where there was "no place to put it."

WHEN I turned 21, I got my first wristwatch—a nice, self-winding Omega—for my birthday. But, after just a few weeks, the minute hand fell off and it had to be sent from New Zealand to Australia to be repaired. It came back just before I set off on a sea draft to Antarctica as a part of my compulsory military training with the Navy. The watch stopped on the voyage south and I "dropped" it into McMurdo Sound one day while we were watching orcas chase Adele penguins through the crystal-clear water. I presume it's still there. I never missed it.

Instead, I got quite good at estimating time, picking it up from public clocks and reading it from the moods and activities of the people around me—it's amazing how governed by routines life can be, and how visibly they're obeyed. I came to never think much about what time it was. As a journalist, I found it freed me to notice other things, some more helpfully than others. Despite this, I usually managed to turn up the recommended five minutes early for appointments—the idea was that it sometimes got you a few extra minutes of interview.

For several years, we lived off the national grid in New Zealand: no electricity or indoor plumbing. And, thanks to some basic celestial navigation training and a general interest in non-European methods of navigation, I got so I could tell the time to within a few minutes from the lay of the stars at night. The stars are a big pattern that appears to revolve each night around the axis of the Earth's poles, and tips to the north or the south a bit as the seasons cycle. So, given enough clear nights, hints of the horizon and practice, you can start guessing the month as well as the time.

This is the sort of time that Virgil would have known: our ancestors were undoubtedly more familiar with the stars than electric light allows us to be.

In much the same way as stars tell time, they'll tell you where you are. That's what celestial navigation's all about. It's a method that's long been known to many cultures. This is primeval time: it makes you very aware of the cycling of things, the unstoppable turning of the solar system and the enormous implacability of the Universe. It's infinite but it is also local and it locates us, not least as human beings: as sentient creatures that gaze upwards to find patterns and to wonder.

THEN, on impulse, I bought a watch from an airline's in-flight catalog.

I'd started travelling a lot with my job, trotting into one time zone after another. It made it harder to dead-reckon local times. So I bought a $50 wristwatch that had no numbers, just little silver notches on a black face. It had an hour hand, a minute hand and one of those 60 jigs-a-minute second hands.

There was also a little window to show the date but the numbers were too small for me to ever read. Without numerals on the face, I found I didn't have to re-set the hands, a fiddly job: I just had to remember which silver sliver marked the "top." In Canada, it was the one opposite the winder; in New Zealand my notional "XII" was the one usually associated with "2." Italian time was the same as New Zealand, the difference being night and day. And I read the "minute" hand's track from the conventional "12."

It confused other people, but it kept me connected with friends wherever they were—sort of like having Facebook on my wrist without the selfies. It was a "Heavens! Is that the time already?" kind of watch. Somewhere, I lost it.

> In Scotland, I regularly travelled by train between Falkirk and Glasgow. Scotrail posted timetables at all of the stations, but I soon found that it could be hard to know whether the train appearing around the bend was the earlier train running late or the scheduled train arriving roughly on time. "Leaves on the line" was the usual explanation for delays. I learned to relax and simply catch the "next" train. Others would look anxiously at their wristwatches or start re-shaping their day's schedules in cellphone conversations with people who should never have expected that these

appointments would slavishly comply with their office clocks. Having relaxed my expectations to suit Scottish commuting, I found travelling in Germany startling. The trains there precisely obeyed scheduled departure and arrival times; the coach doors would close and the train would begin to move … and they'd glide to a halt and the doors would slide open at exactly the scheduled arrival time. I didn't have to read the station signs, just the clocks. I remarked on this punctuality to a German friend, who assured me that the scientists at the national physics laboratory, who regulate the country's standard time signals, set their atomic clocks by watching train departures from the Brunswick Central Railway Station.

DIGITAL clocks seem to despise us. Rather than localizing time, they depersonalize it and, in depersonalizing it, erase our time's ties to place.

They insist that 20 minutes spent in one place are no different from 20 minutes spent in some other place. But times spent in different places are apples and oranges. We'd never naturally bundle them together on the grounds of their duration: it'd be like judging food by the color of the plate.

Digital watches don't "tell" time, they dictate it, they "count" minutes. They have no centre, just numbers that trot pointlessly by as though time were some tiresome universal dimension like length or breadth but with no beginning and no ending—and, therefore, with no meaning. One moment's made equivalent to the next and both are immediately cast into a meaningless numerical past. They give us the "I-never-noticed-I-was-there" experience of time. Virgil would be dismayed.

Digital clocks make me irritable. They misrepresent time as I've come to understand it. With my seventeen "I"s, I knew I couldn't expect things to simply vanish. I knew that experience imprinted itself in my memories and in my emotions; I'd learned that time need not always hustle me on whatever I pass. My past was formed by all those "I"s, "V"s and "X"s, not obliterated by them. Where "is" a digital clock? Where is the centre?

> *A few years ago, my work took me to Bulgaria to write about the bagpiping traditions there. It's music that's extremely difficult to notate. Then, if it is notated, it's almost impossible to play properly from the score because a score can't convey the feeling and spirit of the music, which divides time into moments of human significance. And this music's significance comes about through dance: tempi are overlaid, as the dancers express personal, communal and social relationship. At first, I found it very strange. Then, with a little help from the rakia, I began to hear it, and it became some of the most hypnotically thrilling music I'd ever come across. I'm not insisting that you'd hear it this way, but I am sure that such*

experiences are about, laid like traps of liberation, for all of us. One of the many miracles of life is to bump unexpectedly into something that instantly reveals far more than, left to your own devices, you'd ever have imagined. You can't discipline a search for such moments: they run counter to rational inquiry. But you can be open to them. And they are brought to us, for want of better words, by the angels.

THERE's an excellent book about Bulgarian traditional music by Tim Rice: *May It Fill Your Soul: Experiencing Bulgarian Music*.[10] It goes to the crunch. Music's far more than sounds, notes, modes or scales, and far more than instruments or ensembles. Music's more than a style or a genre. It is about the magical construction of inner human experience. It has to engage and have meaning there if it's going to be heard and not simply shatter silences. And heard, music can touch the whole of life, indelibly.

> *So desperately does our "human condition" cry out for illusions of order in the midst of chaos that it's hard not to imagine time not having something to do with consciousness. Does consciousness need an organizing construct to exist? Without the framework of time, would consciousness fall apart into so many disjointed, passing sensations? Do we imagine time, or music, as a kind of skeleton, a helpful illusion that gives consciousness a form we can experience and utilize? Do we need a concept like time to lift experience from an ocean of chaos and personalize it as a sense of selfhood?*

PERHAPS we'd do well to claim our time—one of our most deeply personal "possessions"—as a medium of creative personal impulse to be shaped, like a sculptor's stone or spread, like a painter's colors, into experiences and expressions of meaning and beauty. That would be a liberating response to its representation as a commodity to be bought or sold.

BUT I have one more clock to mention. In the emergency department of the local hospital I noticed on the wall a clock with Arabic numerals and a second hand that slid around the face with a silent, oily sleekness: no steps or jerks or jumps. It gave me the chilly, creepy feeling that a snake excites as it suddenly uncoils. It was an utterance without punctuation, a representation of a passionless kind of time that waits for nothing and no one; the time that never falters, that offers no pause for reflection, just a seamless form of order with the icy whiff of totalitarianism about it. It was an "I'm-just-passing-through" kind of clock.

Time: A Reflection

IN fact, thanks to the drag of gravity from the Moon and Sun, our Earth's spin is gradually slowing and our days are lengthening. Every few years a second is added to our atom-based "Co-ordinated Universal Time" standard to keep the two measurements synchronized.

time, she rises and sweeps
with a loach-lipped purr
from the room.
in her rippling wake:
a nervous laugh
a sigh
a yawn

a toppled glass
clasps the last light
of hilarity
cups it
and starts to sing
of words
unspoken
of hearts
unbroken

but, ah—
the slow flames of music dance
so much more prettily now
Now that she's gone.

3
Economics and the Artless Bystander

SIGNS AT ENTERPRISE, ONTARIO

IN 1992, "the economy, stupid" were words that helped to get Bill Clinton elected president of the world's most powerful nation. And, despite the so-called financial crisis of 2008 (more accurately, a moral crisis), banging on about the economy can still win over voters, as though a politician's control over big money is any more direct than that of groundhog's shadow in Punxsutawney, Pennsylvania, on the approach of spring.

But why?

BY all sorts of standards, our economic systems are engines of social fracture and environmental damage, resource wastage, injustice and even war.[11] They encourage equanimity where there ought to be outrage, and outrage where we ought to find expectations of justice. Even 2,600 years ago, the Athenian poet and lawmaker Solon was railing against the greed and hubris of his fellow citizens: "even the earth, mighty mother of the gods," had been enslaved, he complained.[12]

In 2015, the International Monetary Fund called income disparity the "defining challenge of our time" and said policymakers should be focusing on the poor and the middle class. "Specifically, if the income share of the top 20 per cent (the rich) increases, then GDP growth actually declines over the medium term, suggesting that the benefits do not trickle down. In contrast, an increase in the income share of the bottom 20 percent (the poor) is associated with higher GDP growth. The poor and the middle class matter the most for growth via a number of interrelated economic, social, and political channels."[13]

COULD better times be in store? Here's the famous pioneering economist John Maynard Keynes writing back in 1928 about life on Earth a century later (i.e., 2028). By then, he projected, overflowing surpluses would meet everyone's needs and we'd face our ultimate problem: "how to use [our] freedom from pressing economic cares, how to occupy the leisure, which science and compound interest will have won for [us], to live wisely and agreeably and well.... I feel sure," he wrote, "that with a little more experience we shall use the new-found bounty of nature quite differently from the way in which the rich use it to-day, and will map out for ourselves a plan of life quite otherwise than theirs."[14]

EAGER to track this Keynesian promise, I dipped into the ideas of 1976 Nobel Prize laureate Milton Friedman about monetary truth and beauty but I found little in pre-handover Hong Kong that I'd want to emulate. Nor could I bring myself to prefer economic "freedom" over social and cultural "freedom."

IN a 2014 lecture at the Royal Academy, Copenhagen, the French anthropologist Bruno Latour told his audience that "as Karl Marx would have said, the realm of transcendence has been fully appropriated by banks.... The world of economy, far from representing a sturdy down-to-earth materialism, a sound appetite for worldly goods and solid matters of fact, is now final and absolute."

And the consequences of thinking in capitalistic terms, he said, are "for most of people who don't benefit from its wealth, a feeling of helplessness and, for a few people who benefit from it, an immense enthusiasm together with a dumbness of the senses. So, when we use capitalism to interpret what is going on, we obtain, on the one hand, binding necessities from which there's no escape and a feeling of revolt against them that often results in helplessness and, on the other, boundless possibilities coupled with a total indifference for their long-term consequences."[15]

So, sacrifice on the altars of the economy, kneel at the shrines of capitalism—then close your eyes, hold your breath and try as hard as you possibly can to believe that everything will be just fine. It's like Imperial Rome: once you'd sacrificed to Caesar "for the safety of the Empire," you could worship any other god you fancied.

It's a clever ruse: freedom on the end of a chain. Celtic druids and early Christians were not the only ones who lost their lives for not playing along. The economy, as a controlling belief system that's not to be messed with, is comparable—in the spirit of which the guidebook of the 1933 Chicago Century of Progress Exhibition carried this chilling motto: "Science finds, industry applies, man conforms."

> *DRIVING on Scotland's West Highland Way, Sue and I saw a small, secluded loch: a perfect place to enjoy our picnic lunch on this sunny, pretty day. We parked and found an inviting place to unpack and eat our sandwiches on a low rise beside the water. We lay back in the silence and stillness. A sudden explosive roar shook the ground and stiffened the water. Time fell apart and three military jets in close formation exploded into our reverie, skimming low and close enough for us to clearly see the helmeted pilots in their cockpits. At eye-level for an instant, they vanished behind a bend in the loch. We were petrified. Had we been in their missile sights, we'd have been ripped apart in the terror we only glimpsed: a terror of the sort that's inflicted almost routinely on the villages and encampments of the underfed and angry aliens we deem "terrorists." Why are we so perennially at war?*

IN January 1964, U.S. President Lyndon Johnson declared war on poverty. For a decade, rates of poverty in the world's richest country were notched back: from 17.3 percent to 11.1 per cent by 1973. But rich folks forgot what good it was supposed to be doing and the policies were pulled.

So, in 2013, UNICEF found, in a ranking of child well-being across 29 "developed countries," that the four places at the very bottom of the table were taken by three of the poorest countries in the survey—Latvia, Lithuania and Romania—and by one of the richest: the United States.[16]

Ironically, poverty doesn't come cheap. A careful study in the U.S in 2008 concluded that child poverty—through lost productivity and economic output, the elevated costs of crime and health care and the lowered value of health—was draining about $500 billion a year from the economy, an amount equivalent to nearly four per cent of gross domestic product.[17] But, despite its outlandish price tag, poverty is allowed to linger.[18]

One obstacle is that consumerist capitalism favors the sorts of interaction that overwhelm cultural values, that structurally favor the rich, the powerful and the well-armed, and that encourage the centralization of wealth and power, locally, nationally and globally. Planet-wide access to resources and markets (through instruments like free trade agreements) only amplifies pressures towards cultural conformity and social subjugation.

> Between 1998 and 2001, Ross McDonald, a researcher at the University of Auckland, New Zealand, paid visits to the Solomon Islands to study the impacts of the global economy on island life. "For most people I met in the islands, and especially for the elders and custom chiefs, the ruthlessness of the forces that are now knocking on their doors is difficult to comprehend," he wrote. "That incoming foreigners would promise more benefit than they ever intended to deliver is, to a society where a person's word is his or her literal honor, an unthinkable ploy....
>
> "In custom, as conceived by many Melanesians, working together for mutual benefit is the only way to meaningful living. Robbing another blind for purely personal gain represents a stunted and immature attitude and a failed spirit: sheer unfamiliarity with the cynical calculations of the many interests now at work in the islands means that some communities have failed to be suitably skeptical of the promises made. However, there are others who see quite clearly what is at stake and recognize the profound differences that lie like a gulf between the customary view of life and the approaching capitalist one. The islands offer many examples of communities trying to contain the temptations of fast money within a more co-operative ethos."
>
> The Islands' traditional co-operative economy was "built upon the twin principles of free labor and shared profits," he observed. For the modern-day followers "of spirit men and prophets in the great Melanesian tradition," as for many in the islands, "money is seen as having an almost magical power to blind a person to traditional common sense. It is obvious to most who live from the forests and the lagoons that these are essential resources, basic to the viability and well-being of the collective. To lose this bounty is to lose everything and no flash-in-the-pan spending spree on trucks or outboards or houses is worth the community dissolution that will inevitably follow."[19]

ANOTHER ace lingers up capitalism's sleeve: the enormous resources and debilitated peoples of sub-Saharan Africa, where life expectancies are half those of most wealthy Western states.

So far, capitalism in places like the Democratic Republic of the Congo—where weapons, deprivation and gang violence have erased all evidence of democracy, republicanism or government—has created a brutal, low-grade war zone where poverty and violence are the intractable norms.

In her 2011 book *Damned Nations*,[20] Canadian doctor Samantha Nutt traced the causes back to such close-to-home activities as pension fund investment policies in Canada that lubricate the enterprise of weapons manufacturers. Financial networks implicate us all in the evils that accompany the exploitation of critical resources in vulnerable countries. Slavery, colonialism, blood diamonds and the rest of it have been but ravens' pecks: the last, great, overwhelming intrusion is being called "development."

In 2010, a vast infrastructure development plan—the Programme for Infrastructure Development in Africa (PIDA)—was launched by the World Bank. It involves road building, communications enhancement and dam building for power generation and irrigation. It aims to add 500,000 to 100,000 kilometres of arterial roads to the resource-rich continent's infrastructure. It's also adding 250,000 kilometres of new or upgraded secondary roads and 70,000 kilometres of rural connecting roads as well as boosting private sector involvements. Funded by international banks, governments and development agencies along with African governments, the aim is to meet these targets by 2040. Then the mining companies, lead players in all of this, will be let loose on the coveted resources embedded in one of Earth's dwindling natural vastnesses. This will compromise wildlife and traditional cultures but, provided that the returns are spread around and the projected benefits reach rural farmers and the region's scattered communities, poverty could be widely and decisively reduced. The roads could bring peace and normality to some of the world's most violently stricken areas.

In 2015, the World Bank's *Africa Pulse* information bulletin noted that sub-Saharan Africa's growth would slow down with falling commodity prices.[21] "Weakening terms of trade present headwinds for the region's commodity exporters; gains for importers." It also said "the rise of new types of conflict and the potential for disease epidemics are risks to the region's prospects." The Ebola epidemic pointed to weaknesses in the health systems of the region. *Africa Pulse* had previously observed that the region's progress in reducing poverty had been slow, "hindered by high inequality." Faster poverty reduction would need greater social equity.

> *WE see a bee, a butterfly, a beetle, a wasp, a fly. It's taking nectar from a flower. It's also spreading the flower's pollen. We're witness to a relationship that's been going on, as you see it today, for 100 million years or more. And, in sustaining itself, the insect is sustaining the plant. In fact, through its ancestors, it's played a hand, not only in giving us substances like beeswax and honey, but also in the plants' evolution, spurring on the diversities of beauty and abundance we see, smell and taste among flowering plants and their fruit. Few of the fruit or vegetables we enjoy could have formed without a pollinator. Moreover, all of these good things have long ignited human inspiration: a kind of spiritual and crea-*

tive pollination. Of course, it can all be explained scientifically. But, when we look for "meaning" instead of "explanation," we find that the whole is greater than the sum of its parts. Everything is benefitting. Here are organisms we seldom give passing thought to that, in sustaining themselves, benefit us all and, apart from the odd sting, harm no other creature. We've fallen into a dangerous place where, in sustaining ourselves, we damage our planet. We impoverish, dupe and damage each other and each others' cultures: we surround ourselves with "collateral damage." Perhaps we'd do well to be more open to the teachings of the beauty and abundance that surround us?

HERE's another story:

It begins as Britain was entering what became known as the Regency period and, with it, the dawn of liberalism: Rousseau and Edmund Burke, Wordsworth and Coleridge, grandiosity, extravagance, high ideals and bloody brutality ... bare-knuckle boxing, public executions, bull-baiting, cock fighting, gambling, dandyism, and a new game called cricket. The newly independent American states were hammering out a constitution; France was emerging from the Terror, and the Napoleonic era was about to begin. The industrial revolution was pawing at the starting gates and shopping was becoming a recreational pursuit.

Britain was one of Europe's most powerful and prospering nations. A burgeoning middle class was enjoying the fruits of trade abroad and industrialization at home. "Disposable" income was giving a new middle class opportunities to explore exotic delights, refine their tastes and pursue the frivolities of fashion and affectation. It was the dawn of modern consumerism.

One popular pursuit was the acquisition of Chinoiserie: vividly glimmering Chinese silks, fine, limpid-green jade, tea and near-transparent porcelain to sip it from. Tea consumption in Britain had reached about 3,000 tonnes a year, and there were hopes that China would soon become a market for Britain's growing industrial surpluses.

The stumbling block was the Qing government. It allowed trading only at the port of Canton and only through the hands of a small guild of licensed merchants, the Cohong. They had little time for "foreign devils" and less taste for their coarse, factory-made goods. They would accept some Indian cotton, sandalwood and medicinally propitious *beche-de-mer* (sea slug, or "sea cucumber"). And they would happily accept silver. But British reserves of silver were running low.

Along the way, a worthwhile niche opened in China for furs. Then, in the mid-eighteenth century, Russians trading sea-otter pelts from Siberia into northern China became the first to realize that Chinese furriers had found a way to selectively remove the long, stiff guard hairs from raw seal pelts without harming the soft, wearable fur beneath. And they knew how to turn inferior furs into felt, so a market began to open for sealskins.

The Americans caught on in 1776, when Cantonese merchants happily paid unexpectedly high prices for a shipment of 13,000 sealskins. The British were quick to follow. Suddenly, the rush was on to ship sealskins to China, load up in Canton with precious Chinoiserie and cut a handsome profit back home in London.

Along remote and rocky shorelines around the Earth, wherever they were known or found to breed, the seals were surprised and slaughtered. The sooner the ships could fill their holds, the shorter the voyage and the surer the returns. An expert sealer, it was said, could rip the pelts from 600 seals in an hour. Seals were taken first by the tens of thousands and then by the hundreds of thousands.[22]

Seals are shy creatures and their breeding colonies had been scattered plentifully around some of the Pacific Ocean's most remote and least hospitable shores. In many cases, indigenous communities, to whom the seals were a vital source of subsistence in otherwise sparse landscapes, had long harvested the seal populations with care and restraint. But the sealers' violent assaults obliterated the colonies. And with the sealers came new diseases. And rats: European ships notoriously introduced black and brown rats—*Rattus rattus* and *Rattus norwegicus*—wherever they touched land.

The real profits of sealing went to speculative ship owners and masters but even an ordinary deckhand might, with a bit of luck, be able to buy the freedom and security of a small farm after a few trips.

In 1796, a fur dealer in London worked out how to rid the pelts of their guard hairs and a market for sealskins opened in Britain too. As seals got harder to find, the long haul to China made less sense. It was more profitable to auction the skins in London.

By the time a British naval lieutenant, William Broughton, charted the Chatham Islands near the subantarctic extremity of the South Pacific, sealing had peaked. It was not until perhaps 15 years later that sealers first stormed ashore on beaches of one of the world's last unravaged sealing grounds. Soon there were scores of them, there to rush the islanders' carefully conserved seal colonies, killing and flaying as many seals as quickly as possible and leaving the carcasses to stink on the shore.

To finish off the broken colonies, captains landed shore parties whose work included growing potatoes and raising pigs to re-provision the ships. They used their guns to hunt shorebirds for a change of diet and, inured to fear and violence, amused themselves by beating or raping the islanders (the *Moriori, t'chakat henu,* people). Their dogs, cats and pigs scavenged, scaring off the ducks and rail that had long been a food source.

As well as seeing their precious food resources laid waste, the Chatham Islanders fell victim to introduced illnesses: in four years, between 1828 and 1832, measles and influenza scythed the population from more than 2,000 to about 1,600.

Well might the Chatham Islanders have retaliated.

In New Zealand, Maori warriors had clashed with and killed disorderly sealers.

The *Moriori* could have killed some of the more obnoxious new arrivals with impunity. But they'd adopted a law that forbade killing: the Law of Nunuku.

Nunuku was a chief who'd realized the social cost of bloody clashes, amplified by the marginal environment of the islands' small land area. He called on the islanders to reject mortal combat and—uniquely as far as anyone knows—the people of this Polynesian warrior culture foreswore violence and destroyed their weapons. Killing ended, so persuasive was Nunuku's influence.

So, for the most part, the *Moriori* did their best to avoid the sealers, getting on with their own lives in their own way. And, with the seals all but exterminated, they might have expected the depredations to end.

But, in the bloody wake of the sealers came whalers, questing the world's oceans for blubber to render into lamp, stove and machine oil, whalebone to nip the waists of fashionable women, ambergris to fix the aroma of their perfumes, and spermaceti for candles, ointments and lubricants. In the Chatham Islands, the whalers found a foul-weather haven right on the edge of the rich Southern Ocean whaling grounds.

In 1835 when the final invasion came—by Maori warriors aided and abetted by whaling captains—nearly 1,000 Moriori, including 160 local chiefs, gathered at the sacred ground of Te Awapatiki, a low-lying point on the main island, and for three days debated the options facing them. Younger leaders were keen to set aside of the Law of Nunuku and wipe out the Maori warriors who, though they might be more experienced and better armed, were still recovering from their crowded passage from Port Nicholson. It could be done. The invaders could be annihilated. Older, highly respected chiefs, imbued with the *mana* of rank, age and ancestral wisdom, spoke for the traditions that formed and held together the fabric of the islanders' universe. To break the Law of Nunuku would be to sever a vital thread in that pattern: their world would fall apart as the *mana* drained from it.

With a deliberation still daunting in its courage and calm resolve, the Chatham Islanders heard the arguments and decided collectively that their *mana* must not be compromised. It would be defended in the only way that it could: by obedience to its sources. They would place *mana* above physical survival, and the Law of Nunuku above expedience and natural inclination. They would display their warriorhood by their courage in facing death.

And death it was. Maori warrior tradition required rights of conquest to be asserted through the spilling of blood. In "walking the land" to establish these rights, Maori invaders met no resistance. They cut down 226 Chatham Island men and women, whose names have been recorded, and a number of children whose names were not. Those who remained were enslaved, moved deliberately from their settlements and put to work to feed and establish the Maori invaders and produce surpluses for trade with whaling captains. In 1840–41, the fledgling New Zealand Company settlements at Wellington relied on slave-grown potatoes from the Chatham Islands.

The whaling captains now had a handy Southern Ocean port, blessed with relatively mild winters, where fresh pork, potatoes and other provisions could be had for cash, tobacco, cloth, rum and whisky. The ships—mostly American but also Australian, French and, less often, other nationalities—would anchor off the main community's beach half a dozen and more at a time, rendering and stowing their whale oil and fresh provisions while their boats were kept ready to take any whales that strayed near the anchorage. Ships' doctors fossicked along the shore, knocking gleaming teeth from the bleached skulls of slaughtered Moriori to be recycled in dental plates back home. In 1862, only 101 Moriori survived. The culture that chose not to kill had been smashed.

"What a poor, curtailed, mutilated, sterile world we threaten our descendants with," wrote Scots-born naturalist and farmer Herbert Guthrie-Smith after visiting New Zealand's sub-Antarctic islands in the early 20th Century: "Man and the rat sharing it—fit mates in many ways—in their desperate, deplorable, gnawing energy, in their ruthless destruction of every obstacle."[23]

And the Chinese? Well, after the Qing Dynasty toughened its opposition to the already illegal importation of opium (grown specifically for that purpose in British India as a monopoly of the British East India Company), the British launched a series of military assaults known as the Opium Wars that forced the Qing Dynasty not only to expose its subjects to an unfettered drugs trade but also to hand over the island of Hong Kong as a trading base. The Chinese people were so infuriated by their government's humiliation that they rose against it in 1850 and 1899 and, in 1912, the 268-year-old Qing Dynasty fell. In many ways, this set the scene for the ascendancy of Mao Zedong, Chinese communism and modern China.

It all made good economic sense. And to think …

It may all have begun with a cup of tea.

> *"THE WEST" is a superpower that's far more intrusive than the old "classical" empires of Greece and Rome. Embedded in its myth is the old promise of a superior destiny: "civilization"—"us." Predominantly English-speaking, white and "rational," we preach "progress" and "globalization" with imperial zeal, elevating principles like "liberalism," "self-regulating markets" and "globalization" to equivalence with Rome's gods and humanity's natural destiny.*
>
> *But we're haunted by an old, inescapably repeated spectacle: Empires fall. All Empires. They follow a trajectory that's fixed by human limitations.*
>
> *An empire's founded on an idea that's vivid enough to ignite a furnace of thought and imagination: innovation, courage, art, philosophy, strategy, weaponry, coercive violence and administrative methodology, myths and narratives. Wealth is imagined, generated, seized and accumulated. But the elite it raises, with minds rarefied by wealth, is purblinded: seeing the awe but not the disappointments of its structures. At the base, alienation and inspiration begin to look alike. Blind to the flaws, the elite instead sees a need*

for control, and ambition dwindles to greed. Corruption makes systems sluggardly. Proliferating complexities at ground level become less intelligible, then beyond control. Fear obstructs effectiveness. Ideals wither. And, when the "barbarians" breach the walls and look around, they wonder what all the fuss was about.

THEN there's Abraham Gesner, the Nova Scotian who transformed the world.

After surviving several shipwrecks, he gave up his youthful dreams of trading horses to the West Indies and, in 1824, married Harriet Webster, the local doctor's daughter. He decided he'd try his hand at a medical career too.

He studied and graduated in England and practised in Nova Scotia, but got sidetracked by an eccentric passion for geology. He mapped the iron and coal deposits of his native Nova Scotia, then those of neighboring New Brunswick where he became the provincial government's first official geologist. With specimens he'd collected around New Brunswick, he set up Gesner's Museum of Natural History—Canada's first public museum. He next got interested in electricity and designed a machine to wrap wire with insulating thread. His interests further widened to include the properties of hydrocarbons. And all of this passionate curiosity saw his indebtedness mount.

He was nearly 50 years old when the slow distillation techniques he was applying to oil shale, coal and bitumen yielded a flammable liquid he named kerosene. He demonstrated it for the first time on 19 June 1846, in a public lecture he gave on "calorifics" in Charlottetown, Prince Edward Island. A few years later, he'd moved to Halifax where, through his lecturing, he'd met up with the septuagenarian Thomas Cochrane, tenth Earl of Dundonald, former governor of Newfoundland and commander-in-chief of the Royal Navy's North American and West Indies Station. Cochrane became a staunch Gesner fan and had the means to help him pursue his ideas.

In 1853, Abe Gesner moved on to New York and, with business partners there, launched the Asphalt Mining and Kerosene Gas Company to recoup the costs of his research. In 1854 he secured U.S. patents 11,203, 11,204, and 11,205 for "improvement in kerosene burning fluids" that he called "A," "C," and "B" kerosene. "A" kerosene was the lightest fraction, later called "volatile hydrocarbon" and, now, "gasoline." "B" kerosene was less volatile, intended mainly for blending with other two grades. "C" kerosene was a lamp fuel soon to be known as "coal-oil" or "carbon-oil."

Until then, household lighting had depended for the most part on smelly tallow candles made from rendered beef and sheep fats. Spermaceti, a wax extracted from the heads of sperm whales, was another option. The Industrial Revolution had increased demand for tallow and whale oil to make soap and to lubricate machinery.

So, with kerosene to replace the costlier and altogether less pleasant sources of household light, the Age of Oil was born, whales were allowed to inch back from the brink of extinction and Abe Gesner returned to Halifax to become a professor of natural history at Dalhousie University. He died there in 1864 at the age of 66.

Harriet had borne him 11 children, four of whom died young: three in infancy and one, Robert, when he was six. One son, George, would stay on in the oil business. He eulogized his dad as a "morning person." The doctor, he wrote, "had black eyes, which shone brilliantly when he was excited, or in earnest conversation." He was a regular churchgoer who relaxed in the evening with his family by playing Scottish tunes on his flute or violin, or enjoying a good cigar.

George illustrated his dad's geniality with a story about a Sunday School picnic in the church grounds, which were surrounded by a high board fence. The pupils were enjoying the day, when "a great band of waifs from the street" mobbed on the other side of the fence, "clamoring for something to eat." The good Doctor Gesner "had a barrel well packed with provisions thrown over the fence to the great delight and satisfaction of those outside ... as it broke on the ground and scattered its dainties far and wide."[24]

Harriet would die several years after Abe, back in the village of Tarrytown, New York, where she'd been born 68 years previously.

The Age of Oil was, at that time, in its infancy. Natural seepage had long brought tar and thick oil to the surface in many parts of the world. Mostly, it was a nuisance. Native people had told Texan settlers the stuff had medicinal properties but ranchers were nonetheless "mighty aggervated" whenever their well-drilling efforts spilled sticky, black, toxic gloop over their pastureland instead of the water that they and their cattle desperately needed.

The earliest attempts to exploit the gloop failed for want of demand. The new fuels only got exciting in the early twentieth century, after a hydrocarbon-fuelled internal combustion engine began putting powered carts and vehicles on the road. Karl Benz in Germany had patented an "auto-mobile" in 1866, but "cars" became widely available only after Henry Ford put his relatively affordable Model T (nicknamed the "Tin Lizzie") on the market in 1908, launching a manufacturing revolution that over 20 years turned out 15 million vehicles—and made the tedium of assembly lines and mass production a global industrial norm. In the meantime, the First World War launched internal combustion engines into the air and, at sea, ships' steam turbines began burning cheap, viscous, violently polluting bunker oil instead of coal ... and then came the marine reciprocating diesel engine. The 1920s saw the boom in road transport beginning to eclipse rail. Unprecedented billows of nitrogen oxides, sulfur dioxide, and particulate matter were being propelled into the atmosphere. It was at that point that the oil and auto industries were positioned to take over civilization.

Coal, the fuel of the steam age, hasn't gone away: it's a massive worldwide source of energy and contributor to climate change to this day. But it's cars and trucks that have changed society most dramatically. Because of oil, we inhabit different realms of experience. Faster travel has sped life up and transformed our appreciation of distances. We have less time to think and feel. Encased in our cars, we see little, hear little, smell little and meet few other people—most of it rushes past too quickly and too far away. If we start riding around in "intelligent" self-driving vehicles, we'll be even further distanced. Walking, we're alive to our senses; there are smells and sounds and small delights to see. Driving, we mesh our senses with the machine: we set the temperature, we choose what we'll listen to, we can talk, we can eat, we can be entertained. And we do it all sitting down in private vulnerability to obesity. Walking, we experience weather immediately and directly, on our skins, and there are people to meet. We're much more limited in what we can carry with us. Riding a horse, as our wealthier ancestors did, the traveller's intimacy with weather and whereabouts and sense of contextual identity weren't greatly compromised. But cars and buses, trains and trucks and every other form of road traffic annihilate it. By and large, modern urban humanity can inhabit a filtered, nature-excluding partial world. Now, instead of ponderous passenger liners, jet aircraft flit us from continent to continent. We measure distances in hours and minutes rather than days, weeks or months. And the olden perils and anxieties of travel have been erased from our daily experience. Transatlantic migrants in the days of sail not only experienced bracing cold and wet, dreadful food and crowded squalor but also faced significant risks of disease and death during the crossing. The worst we can reasonably expect is a delayed flight or "lost" luggage.

A vital element in the transformation of travel has been "HMA": hot-mix asphalt. As old roadways were widened and new roads were built at a rapidly increasing pace, road-building methods changed, stepping up demands for tar. Asphalt had been known for centuries as an occasional paving material and as a water-proofing sealant. It was used here and there in North America to cover small areas of road and walkways from the 1860s. But, as demands for crude oil's lighter distillates for fuels soared, so did the availability and by-production of tarry residues: perfect for road building... and suburban development.

New ways of life sprang up around city perimeters: the commuter became a lead character in the cast of "modern" human life forms. Urban commuters in Canada favor their cars, typically spending an hour or so a day alone travelling a distance of, say, 60 kilometres in a car capable of travelling twice that average speed. What's more, multiple car ownership has become a family norm in many parts of the wealthier West and a major component of the cost of living.

Most of that travel-potential functions a long way below its capacity. Yet, according to the World Health Organization, traffic kills about one and a quarter million people a year, mostly men. It also constitutes a formidable environmental threat.

Parking is the big problem: by 2014, 54 per cent of the total global population was "urban." Car-friendly malls and "supermalls" have degraded old urban economies and countless cities and towns have become less self-sustaining and more difficult to service and manage. Urban slums have grown and rural communities have dwindled as increased mobility and oil-fuelled technology reduced famers' needs for manual labor.

Apart from the enormous role that oil products have come to play as fuels and lubricants in transportation and heating systems, and the direct impacts they've had on our lives, the twentieth century saw enormous growth in the petro-chemicals industry: plastics, synthetic fabrics and fibers, pharmaceuticals, soaps and detergents, fertilizers, pesticides.... All these oil derivatives, unknown a hundred years ago, now turn up almost everywhere in our lives.

Now that we've become so deeply dependent on it, oil wields its own political power. The richest regions of the World owe a lot of their wealth and power to petroleum. But, like all genies that get greedy, that power is turning into a liability, and comes with massive consequences.

> We bend time around our purpose
> like a smith ringing iron at his anvil
> then quench what we forge from our dreams
> in the black, hissing waters of alien realms.
> Stark worlds of difference set apart
> our dreams from the things that we craft
> then see jarringly hefted in others' hands.
> And we yearn to believe it's our time
> at the anvil that counts.
> Death's personal, a minor bodily function;
> Life's communal and rushes on regardless
> to meet again, like mountain cataracts
> reaching the sea, water to water, life to life,
> where all that's been carried or confining
> escapes into the heaving vastnesses;
> and consternations, fears and prides
> in darkening stillness settle
> to silent sediments below.
>
> Freedom's
> learning to drown
> in the wholeness of humanity.

Abe Gesner ... what would your mother have said!

A SMALL corner store in rural Ontario.... I enter as usual to buy the daily newspaper. "The jackpot's $43 million this week," I'm told: this, instead of the usual "good morning." It's a pointer to Lottery Canada's "Lotto Max" mega-prize. I've never bought a lottery ticket: a sudden influx of big money would ruin the life I love. Money's allure, habit-forming small occasional wins, excitement, social affirmation—these are the kinds of drivers that researchers have identified behind the gambling impulse.[25] They can be *compelling, even destructive. And they're applied by gambling promoters with calculated finesse.* Unfairly, lottery "play" functions as a tax on the poor: people who buy weekly tickets imagine an escape from the bleakness of poverty. And all are drawn into accepting greed as a normal human emotion when it's demonstrably deviant. But, if we constantly fan each other's greed, and the society we live in ardently promotes it, it's hard to question the "luck" of the super-rich. Our greed pulls moral curtains over theirs. We do this in a state of suspended sense and reason. Less than half of Lotto Max's sales receipts go into the prize fund. Lottery Canada's website tells you which numbers have turned up most and least often in prize-winning sequences, where winning tickets have been bought, and all sorts of other intentionally distracting factoids chosen to lure gamblers into ever-darker zones of innumeracy. According to Lottery Canada,[26] you stand less than a one chance in 25 million in of winning a lion's share (90 per cent) of the Lotto Max jackpot or a "Max Million." One in 25 million is a bit like hitchhiking blindfold and finding yourself dropped off on a particular 10-acre block of land somewhere in Ontario... anywhere in Ontario, from James Bay to the U.S. border, from the shores of Lake Erie to Ottawa. Yet, in the week before the 9 October 2015 draw, Canadians poured more than $39 million into Lotto Max. It paid out $9.4 million, spread like lard scrapings among just over a million "winners." Meanwhile, lots of people resent paying taxes ... even though taxes offer a far better overall rate of return.

SPEAKING of gambling, there are the stock, commodities and foreign exchange markets; the common shareholder and the very uncommon chief executive officer.

In 2013, chief executive officers of big American companies could comfortably expect base salaries of $1.2 million. Incentive payments added $2.3 million to that and long-term incentives ("LTI's") bumped the total up to $11.4 million. And more than 60 per cent also had free personal use of the company's jet. Canada's highest-paid CEO, John Chen, took home more than $89.7 million in 2014. Citing a study by the liberal Economic Policy Institute, the *New Yorker*'s financial writer, James Surowiecki, pointed out that, since 1965, the pay of big company CEOs had climbed from 20 to 270 times that of their "typical" employee. For that steady rise he paradoxically blamed the publication of that ratio, a requirement introduced by the Securities Exchange Commission that was intended to brake escalating CEO pay. Companies, he said, vied with each other to offer "above average" packages, which, of course, kept nudging the "average" upwards.[27] Boards like to amplify their company's perceived value, and a "cheap" CEO doesn't help. On the whole, though, the correlation between CEO pay and company performance has not been breathtaking. But it's shareholders, not board members, who fork out in the end.

THE economy, I used to amiably think, was about distributing necessities wherever they were needed. This would require work, occupying us in meeting each other's needs more fully, more efficiently, more attractively, more effectively, more thoroughly and more thoughtfully, and these enhancements would create surpluses to underwrite our general cultural development. And we'd all get to know one another.

Or something like that. Silly me! I mean ... what's a necessity? A 2006 Pew Research Centre survey found that more than 80 per cent of Americans regarded a car, a washing machine and a clothes dryer as bare "necessities." More than half added home and car air conditioning, a microwave oven, a television set and a home computer to the list. One-third felt a cellphone, dishwasher and cable or satellite television service were personal essentials. Five per cent felt that the badly needed television had to be flat-screen.

> WE should do away with the absolutely specious notion that everybody has to earn a living. It is a fact today that one in ten thousand of us can make a technological breakthrough capable of supporting all the rest. The youth of today are absolutely right in recognizing this nonsense of earning a living. We keep inventing jobs because of this false idea that everybody has to be employed at some kind of drudgery because, according to Malthusian Darwinian theory, he must justify his right to exist. So we have inspectors of inspectors and people making instruments for inspectors to inspect inspectors. The true business of people should be to go back to school and think about whatever it was they were thinking about before somebody came along and told them they had to earn a living.
>
> — R. Buckminster Fuller[28]

THIS takes me back to the canny English "shop boy" that the poet, playwright and satirist Ben Jonson included in a skit he wrote for the opening in 1609 of London's New Exchange in the city's then-trending West End. One of the world's prototype shopping malls, the New Exchange was represented by its financier, Robert Cecil, Earl of Salisbury, as a showcase of art to camouflage its vulgar commercial purpose.

Two thousand years ago, Epictetus said: "Wealth consists not in having great possessions, but in having few wants." So Ben Jonson's sassy "shop boy" cunningly asks shoppers not what they need, but what they lack. The shop's "master" then extols the exotic wonders on offer and, to conclude the sketch, expresses his heart's desire in prayer: "God make me rich, which is the seller's prayer."[29]

Shopping.... It's just like comedian Steve Martin reputedly said: "I love money. I love everything about it. I bought some pretty good stuff. Got me a $300 pair of socks. Got a fur sink. An electric dog polisher. A gasoline powered turtle-neck sweater. And, of course, I bought some 'dumb stuff,' too."

> We're told we can't "afford" to just quit the dumb-stuff addiction that's destroying our life support system through climate change. The economy is apparently too fragile to cope with the necessary self-restraint. And, while we're reeling with the stupidity of that, there's another stupid threat we don't think about very much either. Nobel Prize laureate Stephen Hawking, in the British newspaper The Independent, warned that "there is no physical law precluding particles from being organised in ways that perform even more advanced computations than the arrangements of particles in human brains. One can imagine such technology outsmarting financial markets, out-inventing human researchers, out-manipulating human leaders, and developing weapons we cannot even understand. Whereas the short-term impact of AI (artificial intelligence) depends on who controls it, the long-term impact depends on whether it can be controlled at all."[30] Elon Musk, the entrepreneur behind the private space technology company, Space-X, and Tesla Motors, echoes Stephen Hawking. He sees artificial intelligence as "the great current threat to human survival."

SO I went back to John Maynard Keynes and his kind-old-gentlemanly vision of the happy future that, in his mistaken estimation, should be making itself felt around now: "I see us free, therefore, to return to some of the most sure and certain principles of religion and traditional virtue—that avarice is a vice, that the exaction of usury is a misdemeanor, and the love of money is detestable, that those walk most truly in the paths of virtue and sane wisdom who take least thought for the morrow. We shall once more value ends above means and prefer the good to the useful. We shall honor those who can teach us how to pluck the hour and the day virtuously and well, the delightful people who are capable of taking direct enjoyment in things, the lilies of the field who toil not, neither do they spin."

Perhaps, instead of nurturing expectations of halcyon bliss, we've been overly preoccupied by his dire warning that "for at least another hundred years we must pretend to ourselves and to everyone that fair is foul and foul is fair; for foul is useful and fair is not. Avarice and usury and precaution must be our gods for a little longer still. For only they can lead us out of the tunnel of economic necessity into daylight."

The hundred years is almost up and daylight sounds good—if it means living life to the full, with passion and without fear. So I find it odd to read that "avarice and usury and precaution must be our gods" to bring the dawn, when what we've actually seen—not always, perhaps, but too often—is avarice, usury and precaution leading not to pleasant glades so much as to costly extensions of the tunnel.

Again, it's our preconceptions that hold us back. We reach their boundaries and think we've reached the edges of reality.

> *In a lifeboat lingered seven sailors whose ship had gone down in a storm. After several long nights of dread, with the last of their food gone, they found their boat drifting close to a tropical shore, but not one of them could swim. Becalmed, weakened, and without oars or sails or lifejackets, they prayed for a wind that would blow them to the beach. It did not come. Each day, their boat teasingly drifted a little closer to the shore, then a little further from it, to and fro. One by one, the survivors died. Those who lingered began to curse God for His cruelty. The fruit they imagined beyond the beach heightened their anger; they were sure there'd be food there, shellfish on the rocks and flocks of plump birds—thoughts that mocked their starvation. They raged and weakened. The last was a young sailor who'd desperately wanted to see his newborn child. He'd clung to life in that hope. At last, not wanting to die raving and insane as he'd seen his companions die, he hauled himself to the gunwale and, with his last spasm of strength, toppled into the sea expecting to drown. His eyes widened. He was sitting up to his neck on a coral reef.*
> *"Shit," he said.*

This is your story to conclude.
Welcome to the Anthropocene.

4
Cultures of One

BY THE FIUME TEVERE (RIVER TIBER), ROMA, ITALIA

IT'S as silly to expect two people to agree as it is to expect everyone to agree. Don't you agree?

After all, we live in times that celebrate self-defining, self-asserting individualism; we have ever-widening cultural menus from which to piece together a social presence. Online, we can be ourselves or somebody else, or we can enhance ourselves beyond recognition. We can create, combine or co-opt multiple, context-appropriate virtual identities, anonyms, avatars and pseudonyms. Identity can be a plaything. We no longer necessarily know who we're talking to. And we no longer necessarily need to know who we are.

And this is just one aspect of the social change that's all around us.

FOLLOWING the First World War, the fatal weakening or collapse of Europe's great empires and many social shifts launched by Europe's agrarian and industrial revolutions were accelerated. Since then, the impacts of unharnessed human ambition have become so startling that the term *Anthropocene* (the "human age") has been coined to identify a new epoch of planetary change.

The depths and dramas of human achievement in the past century or so include atmospheric, marine, terrestrial and climatic changes, accelerated extinctions and reorganizations of local and global ecosystems. They're nature's adjustments to human forces like grand-scale agriculture, industrialization and urbanization. "We" now face the responsibilities of running the planet or ruining it.

> Here's a widely cited scientists' view from 2010:
> "How have the actions of humans altered the course of Earth's deep history? The answers boil down to the unprecedented rise in human numbers since the early nineteenth century ... linked with massive expansion in the use of fossil fuels....
> "The most plainly visible physical effects of this on the landscape ... may in some ways be the most transient.... Far more profound are the chemical and biological effects of global human activity....
> "Today, the rise in CO_2 to over a third above preindustrial levels has been demonstrated beyond reasonable doubt....
> "The rise in temperatures, that, at high latitudes, already exceed modeled predictions, has important consequences. The fringes of the great polar ice-sheets, once thought to react sluggishly to temperature rises, are now seen to respond quickly and dynamically. The ensuing sea level rise, scarcely begun, may ultimately be of the order of several metres if temperatures rise by some 2°–5° C., as predicted....
> "Global temperature rises will have far-reaching consequences for the biosphere....
> "The ultimate effect ... is a sharp increase in the rate of extinctions. Current estimates put the extinction rate at 100–1,000 times greater than the background level, and the rate is projected to increase by a further tenfold this century. This current human-driven wave of extinctions looks set to become Earth's sixth great extinction event...."[31]

"PROGRESS" strains our capacities to solve or soften the surprise side-effects of previous "progress." Nuclear power is an example. Waste from as far back as the 1950s is still piling up in deteriorating storage tanks at Britain's Sellafield nuclear reprocessing site. Year by year, the risk of calamity grows.

In 2015, the British government fired the private consortium it had hired to clean the site up, gave the job back to a government agency, and pushed the projected completion date ahead from 2120 to 2030. The cost to British taxpayers will top £100 billion.

A similar problem confronts Germany where the walls of the Asse salt mine are buckling. There, 126,000 drums of plutonium-bearing radioactive waste were secretly sequestered in the 1970s. They now need to be relocated. More nuclear waste is piling up in Germany where 17 nuclear plants scheduled for decommissioning by 2022. Demolition debris will add enormously to the stockpile.

Then there's the United States, looking for somewhere to safely store 70,000 metric tons of accumulated spent nuclear fuel, a stockpile to which another 2,000 to 2,300 metric tons are necessarily added each year.

France, Russia, South Korea—all are in similar predicaments. And the ongoing Fukushima disaster cleanup is just starting: it's expected to cost tens of billions of dollars before it's completed sometime in the next 20 to 30 years.

Time and again, we seem destined to chase after "needs" that have been created by our chase after earlier "needs". Meanwhile, the centralization of wealth in the "developed" world and an expanded global population have upped the ante.

THE social changes are fluid and complicated. They take most of us by surprise. They come with redistributed benefits and injuries. And there's no going back.

At the local community level, old landmarks—schools, shops and services, churches, sports and social clubs, libraries and other amenities—have had to rethink their roles and reasons. Many snap and fold. It's not the end of the world, nor the end of "civilization." But, as knock-on effects ripple through the system, they jolt our social habits and sensibilities.

> *When I was a little boy, my mother would often send me down to Frank Graham's grocery store on Selwyn Road to pick up something: a bottle of milk, a pound of butter, a packet of cigarettes or a loaf of bread … that sort of thing. It was a 15-minute walk each way to "get me out of the house".*
>
> *One of my pleasures was to ding the old brass service bell on the counter. The shop was a roadside extension of the Grahams' weatherboard home and, if Frank was away, his wife or daughter would come through from the house to serve. I hoped it would be the daughter. She'd dip into one of the big glass jars of sweets—"Minties" were my favorites—and give me one. Her mother? Never.*
>
> *The smells were wonderful: fresh bread, tea leaves, ice cream and milkshake flavorings, cloth and leather and morning newspapers. A slab of glazed ham sat on the hand-turned slicer. If you wanted something Grahams' didn't have, Frank would take an order and you could pick it up a week later.*
>
> *In the village, local produce seasonally filled the greengrocer's, and the butcher and his brother (maybe it was his cousin) them-*

selves killed the creatures they sold as meat. Each wore a blue striped apron and white cap and had a scarred leather holster on his belt holding a big knife and honing steel. They had a massive, chipped wooden chopping block, a handsaw and a heavy cleaver, and deftly whacked, slapped and wrapped customers' orders from whole sides of mutton and beef. You couldn't buy meat until it had hung in the chiller long enough to darken and tenderize, and the flavors had matured.

Filling an order was often hard, heavy physical work, accompanied by a stream of teasing banter directed at waiting customers. Trimmings went into a mincer and hand-operated sausage-making machine that took the two of them together to manage: filling, twisting and stacking the natural casings into chains of plump sausages.

Food was all around us: fish we could catch off rocks at the end of the beach. Fruit and vegetables came from the village shop or from our own garden. Neighbors exchanged baking and garden harvests. And everyone seemed to have laying hens—"chooks."

In hunting season, although my dad never hunted, there were often ducks and, sometimes, wild pork or deer.

Friday was "late shopping night": the "end of the week." People in the street were happy and talkative. The stores stayed open until 8 p.m.; most would re-open at 9 a.m. on Monday. Motorists carried war-surplus steel jerry-cans full of petrol if they planned to drive far over the weekend.

My dad was an engineer who helped a New Zealand-born Chinese entrepreneur, Tommy Ah Chee, set up Auckland's first supermarket: Foodtown. On the evening of Tuesday, 17 June 1958, we drove out to Otahuhu for a private pre-opening tour as Tom's guests. We were agape: Tommy gave us a cart and told us to find everything we'd usually buy in a week or two and to let him know if there was anything, anything else at all, that we couldn't find on the serried rows of shelving. I seem to recall my mother asking Tom about toothpaste. It was there; we'd missed it. He then insisted that we accept everything we'd picked up as a "thank you" to my dad.

There was something creepy to this: something odd about all the pre-wrapped stuff, and the lettuces: cleaned off and stacked across from cereal cartons, and shoe polish in the same enormous shop as a meat counter.

Tommy died in 2000 aged 72. Six years later, developers uncovered a brick courtyard and fireplace on a site in Auckland they'd identified as his migrant ancestors' original New Zealand home. Their finds included a small hoard of late nineteenth-century

Chinese ceramic shards. It now seems to me that the origins of Foodtown's "food" had similarly been broken and hidden from view. I don't "blame" Tommy for that; he was simply "modernizing."

A decade later, we'd moved to the city. Dad and I got to fish together less often though I'd bring home fish I speared while diving, or shellfish I'd gathered, and our urban garden produced subtropical fruit throughout the year. Bread was still delivered, unsliced and unwrapped, to a box at the gate, and whole milk (the only kind to be had) was home-delivered in recycled glass bottles. But most of our food was now bought in grocery stores. And we could buy cooked "takeaways": fish and chips as a rule, or meat pies (mince or steak), with kidney, onion or mushrooms.

Then I moved to Canada to study. Here, supermarkets were already a well-established norm. "Shops" were for clothes and "stuff": ornaments, hardware and electrical goods. Bookshops were getting scarce and fewer shops remained independent businesses that reflected their owners' quirks and fancies. Most were chain "outlets" with identical stock and even identical layouts, color schemes, lighting and muzak, and one small town started looking pretty much like the next. In more and more medium-sized and larger towns, chain stores were being grouped together in malls. I became aware of needing to remember where I'd parked the car. And, just as a "patient" would soon become a "client" in the idiom of the innocent, individual "customers" became en bloc "consumers," no longer always "right."

A more recent development has been the relative demise of the family meal. Takeaways, drive-throughs and "family restaurants" have jumped the queue on supermarkets and it's often just top-up snacks that come from home refrigerators and cupboards.

In Scotland we saw a family spend an evening together. One by one, family members would individually step out to buy chips for themselves. In Canada, we've been surprised by friends arriving at our home for a meal together with a Tim Horton's cardboard coffee cup in hand. Dammit, we can "do" coffee here at home. One young couple we visited had a kitchen oven still in factory wrapping. It had been in their apartment for a year, never used. They simply lived on takeaways. Our "dinner together" was eaten out of polystyrene boxes on the way back to the apartment.

So the advent of synthetic and artificial food-like products shouldn't be too surprising. They offer cheap, quickly-prepared, multiple meals without the need for varied ingredients, and contain the nutrients needed to sustain life. What could be better? "Soylent" is an example: a powdery "food substitute" that can be stirred together with liquid and turn the socially complicated rituals and creative challenges of dining into a few moments of personal refueling ... and it looks as if it could catch on.

IN our experience of this kind of distancing, yawning income differences and polarized social opportunities are just the brute forces.

They're intensified by generational differences, pressures and personal values.

They're complicated by social media, entertainment, overt sexual orientations, interests, tastes, politics and virtual realities, overflowing as they proliferate, to establish their own, new webs of relationship, pressures, tenets, influences, appetites, priorities, norms, codes and interests. Core life experiences, from child-rearing norms to the nature of work and patterns of consumption, have shifted.

Since the 1990s, technological and social changes have been especially radical, accelerated, invasive and sweeping. New media slam-dunk complexities into the heart of family life. They invite individual members of a single family to privately, independently, indulge their own tastes. Each can now access his or her own information sources, and engage with his or her own social networks in their own virtual realities.

Information flows have changed dramatically. Television—the family gathered around the glowing screen in the living room — is passé. Are there still homes where arguments can be heard about whose hand holds the remote control?

We're seeing "personal space" withdraw from "public space." The construction of condominiums, timeshares, "planned unit developments" and gated communities, with their covenanted "homeowner associations" and security systems—what's called "common interest development" ("hidey-holes" in plain-speak)—has been a booming niche for speculative builders in North America.

IT'S tempting—even necessary—to sometimes step aside and free-fall into the consolations of "comfort zones": space that's less constantly demanding, set apart from the surrounding frenzies. They give us simulations of a life without overwhelming pressure or change and meet day-to-day needs for familiarity.

But they can entangle us in a kind of "freeze-frame" self-image that life's stresses immediately rise against.

And aging can hurt. So, for example, in 2007 at the age of 44, actress Demi Moore (aka Demi Guynes Kutcher), by then married to a 29-year-old third husband and having spent half-a-million dollars on cosmetic surgery—breast implants, collagen injections, liposuction and a procedure to lift the sagging skin on her knees—announced that she'd drawn a line in the sand, and launched a campaign against "ageism" in Hollywood because she was no longer getting $12 million movie contracts.

This particular kind of discrimination has been inflicted especially on women.

For men, the debility's erectile dysfunction. If it lasts three months or more, it's often declared a "clinical condition," despite being a natural result of changes that a non-specialist might sensibly sum up with a three-letter word: "age."

Anti-aging treatments and technologies have become big business. Cosmetic surgery, in the United States alone, was by 2007 a $10-billion-a-year industry. And, more and more, we're seeing once "normal" changes rebranded as pathologies. It's a lucrative form of market extension for the drug companies and for the less sophisticated "health products" industry trailing in their wake with extracts and placebos for sale.

It's also revealed some touching needfulness. In 2009, in support of an anguished woman who, in good faith, had bought Estée Lauder's premium-priced "Tri-Aktiline Instant Deep Wrinkle Filler," the American Advertising Standards Authority banned advertising that claimed the cream made wrinkles vanish "instantly."

Half of the more than 3,300 physicians and scientists who signed up for the Eighth International Congress on Anti-Aging and Biomedical Technology in Las Vegas in 2000 said they expected to live to be at least 120 years old. That would add three or four decades of progressive debility to their lives.

There's a business plan to this. The pitch to exhibitors at the 2014 conference in Orlando, Florida, was that "Americans 50 years of age and older control 77 per cent of the country's financial assets; over the next 10 years, population growth will be driven by a decrease in mortality, not an increase in birth rate; 90 million adult Americans use alternative medicine; Botox was the number one cosmetic procedure performed with 2.8 million procedures, up 157 per cent from 2002," and "the consumer public has voted with their wallets overwhelmingly in favor of the anti-aging healthcare model. The anti-aging marketplace is one that is demographics-driven: people around the world are getting older." [32]

Age, it seems, has become hot property. Forget that it will be a wretched way to live even if you can afford the medication.

GLOBALIZATION and the jarring reverberations it sets up in the social harmonics of those who influence and those who are influenced—rather than drawing us into one great, mutually-appreciative celebration of common humanity—seem to open fissures under our feet. We find ourselves falling too easily into disappointment, alienation, exclusion, despond and isolation. It's mostly self-inflicted, fear being far quicker than curiosity.

> "The most beautiful experience we can have is the mysterious. It is the fundamental emotion that stands at the cradle of true art and true science. Whoever does not know it and can no longer wonder, no longer marvel, is as good as dead, and his eyes are dimmed. It was the experience of mystery—even if mixed with fear—that engendered religion. A knowledge of the existence of something we cannot penetrate, our perceptions of the profoundest reason and

the most radiant beauty, which only in their most primitive forms are accessible to our minds: it is this knowledge and this emotion that constitute true religiosity. In this sense, and only this sense, I am a deeply religious man.... I am satisfied with the mystery of life's eternity and with a knowledge, a sense, of the marvellous structure of existence—as well as the humble attempt to understand even a tiny portion of the Reason that manifests itself in nature."—Albert Einstein[33]

RUSSELL Belk, as Kraft Food Canada Chair in Marketing at York University in Toronto, has studied the meaning of stuff—of possessions, of collecting it and giving it, and materialism.

Back in the 1980s, he described what he called the "extended self": a personal identity consciously self-created by strategic consumption. "Possessions are central to our sense of self," he wrote: "And our relationship with possessions is seldom just a person-thing relationship, but rather a person–thing–person relationship as they connect us to, remind us of, and announce something about us to various other people in our lives."[34] Even he never said whether it'd make us happy.

The stuff-structured relationships that stick most vividly in my mind involve yard sales when we've been on the agitated verge of yet another move. I've done my best to blot them from my memory.

THE boundaries of "selfhood" are drawn differently by different cultures. Expectations and obligations vary depending on one's age, gender, marital and parental status, one's family and associates, one's occupational role and community standing.

Robert A. Paul, a professor of anthropology and interdisciplinary studies, has studied the relationship between our genetic inheritance and our cultural one, finding their impacts not only intimately interrelated but also finding them sometimes in conflict, but also confirming culture as a powerful engine of human diversity.[35]

Obeying conventions and meeting others' expectations have been decisive in leading us to wherever we now find ourselves. Our "selfhood" may have struggled, resisted and followed a few dreams of its own, but it seldom succeeds in freeing us. Flouting the forces of culture can make life difficult and dangerous: there are penalties for defying convention, even in societies as extreme in their individualism as those of the New World. And, when our culture shifts under our feet, we can feel we're failing on several fronts all at once. *Washington Post* journalist Brigid Schulte has described the frenzied lives facing those caught in the midst.[36] She identified anxiety levels among high school students in the 2010s that matched those of 1950s psychiatric patients, and pointed to the health risks of culturally-imposed "role overload."

> Try to remember each ocean wave's
> unfolding, wonderful form ...
> Try to recall the sweet startle
> of each picked berry bitten,
> Try to re-live the grateful rise
> of every in-drawn breath,
> Try to re-wonder the first time
> that the stars shone into your night,
> Try to thrill as when first you rose
> to set off on your way alone,
> Try to sigh as at last you sighed
> when you found your long way home
> Try to dream all your fondest dreams
> over and over again.
> Now look deep in another's eyes
> and release what you feel inside....

LIFE at any age comes with real and imagined anxieties, discomforts and complaints waiting to be pacified by imaginative entrepreneurs.

Avalanches of "self-help" books tap into our rising demand for meaning. Typically they present reworkings of what were originally "religious" insights and practices.

So, for example, in his 2013 book *The Distraction Addiction* Professor Alex Soojung-Kim Pang wrote about the importance of being able to "focus on what's important." He promoted what he called "contemplative computing. Contemplative computing isn't enabled by a technological breakthrough or scientific discovery. You don't buy it. You do it."

He injects a style of language derived from religion into new constructions of thought, emotion, belief and even secular ritual. In sharp contrast with religious emphases on self-discipline, though, Soojung-Kim Pang affirms self-entitlement. His is a wide, diversely expressed and essentially individualistic quest for inner peace that, freed from troubling encounters with "mystery," nevertheless draws elements of old, mainstream religions into its orbit.

So we see American television anchorman and "lifetime non-believer" Dan Harris parleying his media celebrity into book sales with his *10% Happier: How I Tamed the Voice in My Head, Reduced Stress Without Losing My Edge, and Found Self-Help That Actually Works—A True Story.*

It's actually a book about meditation, a discipline that's been around for millennia. It's now a commodity, marketed as a training program for aspiring "achievers."

Walter Mischel, a Columbia University psychology professor, wrote a self-help book about self-control: *The Marshmallow Test: Mastering Self-Control* (Little, Brown). In an interview with *New Scientist* magazine, he spoke about popular culture's assaults on self-control: "We're all open to enormous temptations. Advertising is brilliant at creating temptations that are extremely hard to resist." Widely ignored in research about self-control, he pointed out, have been standards acquired early in life against which we measure our entitlement to indulge ourselves.37

SPEAKING of self-control, how about fasting?

Among Christianity's myriad denominations, fasts have long been observed in various ways. Buddha told his followers that refraining from evening meals made him aware of "good health and of being without illness ... of buoyancy and strength and living in comfort." So Buddhist monks and nuns often forego food after their midday meal.

As well as fasting for festivals, Hinduism encourages more regular fasts, depending on one's preferred manifestations of god. And it's common to fast on the anniversary of a parent's death.

Fasting is one of the defining "Five Pillars of Islam," Ramadan being the best known and most widely observed. As well, Islam encourages other, voluntary fasts. Abstinence is understood to deepen awareness of god and heighten moral awareness, as well as promoting health and wellbeing.

Bahá'í fast from sunrise to sunset during the month of *Ala*. Expectant and young mothers, invalids, people doing heavy physical work and a few others are exempted. Along with prayer, it's one of the faith's greatest obligations.

Biologist Mark Mattson's research at the Laboratory of Neurosciences at the American National Institute on Aging in Baltimore led to the popularization of "intermittent fasting" to reduce the risks of obesity, diabetes, cancer, asthma, cardiovascular disease and neurodegenerative disorders. It helps cells handle stress and resist disease. Fasts seem to lower the risks of stroke, and of Alzheimer's, Parkinson's and Huntington's diseases.

Mark Mattson found intermittent fasting improved glucose regulation, helped trim belly fat without harming muscle mass, lowered blood pressure and promoted the sort of heart rate variability that's seen in endurance athletes.

His work and that of others led to a BBC *Horizon* documentary. *Eat, Fast and Live Longer* was persuasively presented by British media-medic Michael Mosley, who then co-authored a book with fashion and feature writer Mimi Spencer. Popular media spread the word.

A person on the "5:2 diet" eats "normal" amounts of healthy food five days a week, then just one moderate-sized (500–600 calorie) meal on each of the other two days. This is in a world where most people would be delighted to see "normal amounts" of healthy food any day of the week.

Followers of the 5:2 diet are spared the moral and social responsibility that the Jewish prophet Isaiah held to be the core essential of fasting: He proclaimed, on behalf of his god: "This is the kind of fasting I have chosen: to loose the chains of injustice and untie the cords of the yoke, to set the oppressed free ... to share your food with the hungry and to provide the poor wanderer with shelter—when you see the naked, to clothe them, not to turn away from your own flesh and blood."

He detailed the benefits in poetic terms: "If you do away with the yoke of oppression, with the pointing finger and malicious talk, and if you spend yourselves on behalf of the hungry and satisfy the needs of the oppressed ... your light will rise in the darkness, and your night will become like the noonday."

We tend to do stuff like fasting these days in our own way, in the shade, out of the midday sun, and without worrying overly about "yokes of oppression."

GRATITUDE makes you happy too: University of California Davis psychologist Robert Emmons, editor-in-chief of the scholarly *Journal of Positive Psychology*, says so. In his 2008 self-help manual, *Thanks!—How Practicing Gratitude Can Make You Happier*, he promotes the idea that "goodness" exists in the world, some of it independently of oneself. Fostering that awareness, he assures his readers, has been proven in randomized, controlled experiments to cultivate happiness, well-being and healthfulness: "regular grateful thinking can increase happiness by as much as 25 per cent, while keeping a gratitude journal for as little as three weeks results in better sleep and more energy." In 2013, he published *Gratitude Works!: A Twenty-One-Day Program for Creating Emotional Prosperity* (San Francisco: Jossey-Bass).

Gratitude, long expressed in prayer and facilitated by ritual, is now a form of psychotherapy. Resources include the *Gratitude Resentment and Appreciation Test (GRAT)*. Its 44 items evaluate three clinically defined factors: abundance, simple appreciation, and appreciation of others. Pared-down, 16- and nine-item forms also seem to work. A *Gratitude Questionnaire: Six Item Form* asks you how much you agree with statements like "I have so much in life for which to be thankful," "If I had to list everything that I felt grateful for, it would be a very long list" and "I am grateful to a wide variety of people."

The "positive affect" that's generated is thereby distanced from the religiosity that's been transmitting the same insights for thousands of years.

OTHER articles in the *Journal of Positive Psychology* suggest that humility, mindfulness, hope, courage, forgiveness and compassion can also be "good" for us ... if we can cope with all of these fresh demands on our time.

Even the gift to faith that is solitude has received a little—just a little—corollary attention from the self-help industry. In 1988, the late Anthony Storr, an English psychiatrist and author, published *Solitude: A Return to the Self*, which emphasizes the place of solitude in art and creative exploration. It references artists ranging from Beethoven to Beatrix Potter (along with a good bit of Jung) but insists that spending time alone also enriches less extraordinary mortals.[38]

Thirty years previously, the great French-American Catholic writer and mystic

Thomas Merton, spoke out for solitude more bluntly:

> *The murderous din of our materialism cannot be allowed to silence the independent voices which will never cease to speak. It is all very well to insist that man is a "social animal—the fact is obvious enough. But that is no justification for making him a mere cog in a totalitarian machine—or in a religious one either, for that matter. In actual fact, society depends for its existence on the inviolable personal solitude of its members. Society, to merit its name, must be made up not of numbers, or mechanical units, but of persons. To be a person implies responsibility and freedom, and both these imply a certain interior solitude, a sense of personal integrity, a sense of one's own reality and one's ability to give himself to society—or to refuse that gift. When men are merely submerged in a mass of impersonal human beings pushed around by impersonal forces, they lose their true humanity, their integrity, their dignity, their ability to love, their capacity for self-determination. When society is made up of men who know no interior solitude it can no longer be held together by love: and consequently it is held together by a violent and abusive authority. But when men are violently deprived of the solitude and freedom which are their due, the society in which they live becomes putrid, it festers with servility, resentment, and hate.*[39]

AMERICAN author, essayist, and literary critic William Deresiewicz taught English at Yale University between 1998 and 2008. His view is a kind of "Merton-lite": "Religious solitude is a kind of self-correcting social mechanism, a way of burning out the underbrush of moral habit and spiritual custom. The seer returns with new tablets or new dances, his face bright with the old truth."[40]

MANY recoil from this. Researchers at the Universities of Virginia and Harvard found that rather a lot of people prefer physical pain to spending time alone with nothing to do but think.[41] "Most people do not enjoy 'just thinking' and clearly prefer having something else to do," said the study's authors.

AN ISSUE facing those who'd mine religious insights as self-help fixes is the loss of context and re-shaped intention. To find "god" or Nirvana can be rather different from finding ourselves and reconstructing our relationships with life's modern pressures and demands. In a *New Scientist* article in 2015,[42] for example, psychologists Miguel Farias at Coventry University in the U.K. and Catherine Wikholm at the University of Surrey sounded a warning about faddish "mindfulness." They'd found popular media reports heavily biased: "findings of moderate positive effects were inflated, whereas non-significant and negative findings went unreported." They cited studies like that of David Shapiro at the University of California, Irvine, who found that seven percent of people on meditation retreats experienced "profoundly adverse effects including panic and depression." Other studies have found biological stress levels raised and impacts on some forms of learning. Positive effects are often short-lived.

STILL, whatever's said (or sold) about "happy," more than a few potentially game-changing elephants are bumping flanks in the "underbrush of moral habit and spiritual custom."

They're questions about us: who we are and how competent we are to deal with the moral, practical and spiritual implications of such hazards as the globally pernicious impacts of poverty, climate change, environmental degradation, waste, injustice—all of the "collateral damage" that's inflicted by choices we've made or feel compelled to accept. We face many threats alone, but isn't that the way of things?

> *My dad spent four years of his life in Italy. For pretty much all that time, day and might, he was being shot at by German soldiers. One of them finally got him, inflicting a wound inside his left thigh. Had that bullet hit ever so slightly higher and a little to the side, my father would never have been able to conceive me. The wound pained him for the rest of his life. Another time, an artillery shell embedded itself in a clay embankment against which he and a fellow soldier had taken shelter. It roared like a motorbike between their heads, thumped into the clay and failed to explode. Dad always said he owed his life that time to a saboteur in a forced-labour Nazi munitions factory. His "close calls—and there were more of them —were in a very particular sense mine. I would not be born until those dangers had passed. And, had any of them done for my dad, I would not exist. But think about it: everybody's bound to have beaten similar odds at other times and under different circumstances on their long way into existence. And, even having made it this far, we're each of us vulnerable, day-by-day, to unforeseen hazards. The trick, surely, is to make the most of these twists of circumstance and get on with it.*

MAYBE the best we can do is to trust whatever it's been that launched us into this maelstrom of human complexity. And live deeply where, rather than accumulating inducements, compulsions, anxieties and impulses, one's self has the most room to become known, and stretch.

5
Seeking Selfhood

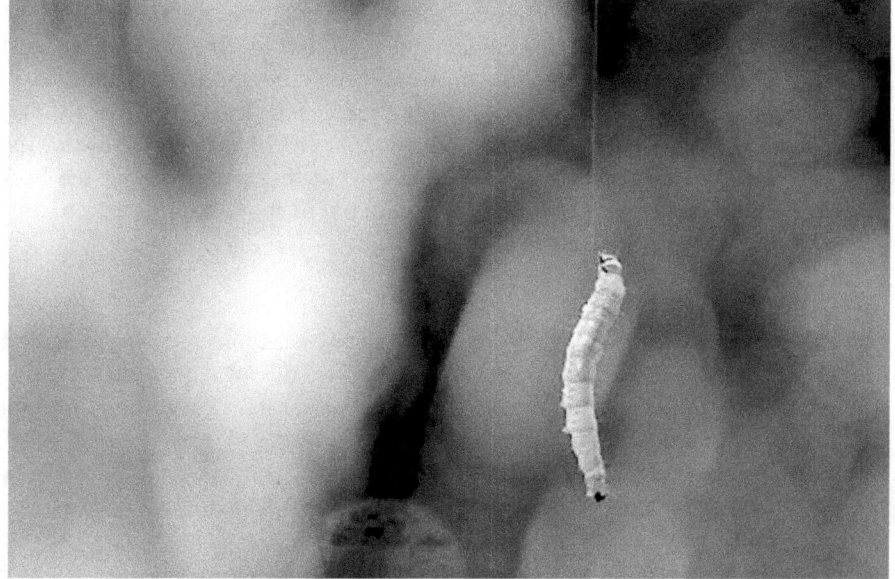

THE CATERPILLAR

I LOVE photographing wildflowers. They can peak and fade in a day but, very often, they have, for just those few hours, displayed a dogged kind of beauty that's jolted me into wider emotions and fresh insight. It had rained and I was walking by the river photographing wildflowers when a little green caterpillar caught my eye. A tiny thing, it was swinging about on a barely-visible thread from a branch 12 feet above my head. I began taking photographs, chasing the focus as it moved this way and that in the barest of breezes. All around, newly emerged dragonflies were gorging on mosquitoes and other small flying things. One peeled off like a jet fighter, brushing my ear as it passed, and the caterpillar was gone. Life over. But I have a photograph. And you have seen it.

WE find large parts of who-we-are among our memories and it's been confidently estimated that our brains can hold around 12,000 gigabytes of data—wow!—but uploading's erratic and storage is neither digital nor reliable.

Our memories have lives of their own. They're flirty and highly-strung. They'll hang out together and chat each other up, they argue and fight and play then run out of reach, popping back into our minds years later. They party and work up each other's emotions ... they'll even make stuff up. They noisily chime in whenever we try to accomplish anything but the simplest and most reflexive of actions. They butt in at bad moments. They can deflate inflated egos and flash-freeze the heat of passion. We don't necessarily like them all that much but, when we start reaching for them, they're quite likely to change their story or leave bits out.

Moreover, memories may make a point of managing our moods, motivations, values and impacts, bunching up around emotional highs or lows, or contorting themselves to fit the structure of a likely story. But they stand, too, at the back door of conscience, as a voice and as an ally. And, if memory is doing its job, we'll know when and why we are doing wrong. Or right.

FRIENDS ... a few, the closest, are for "life", deeply etched into our own identity; others get us through a phase in life. They help us to fill out a particular, passing context, then dissolve into memories of a past we'd not have got through without their help and companionship. They are wholly of a time and place. A few, I know, I failed badly as life carried us apart.

All, though, somehow remain an indelible part of me: the biology teacher who turned my little pram dinghy into a centre-board sailer; the teenage girlfriend — a good and balanced spirit who helped me find myself in the tangle of a teenagehood endured at a bullying, discipline-heavy boarding school. At university there were teachers and close friends, Maori and Polynesian, who opened to me fuller dimensions of cultural, spiritual, geographic and oceanic appreciation. And the beautiful young Japanese woman, a fellow student I had every intention of marrying and with whom I deepened my attraction to cultures other than my own. The "oldest" of my friends remains a Zambian-Malawian New Zealander with whom I've somehow shared a unique closeness since our university days. Life has given me a soul-friend, lover and wife who is Canadian. Work as a writer for Scotland's National Piping Centre engaged me with the world's best bagpipers and exponents of various European traditions, not just in Scotland, but also in Ireland and across Europe ... to Italy and Bulgaria especially. There are people who are or have been neighbors. There are people I've lived or worked among in various ways, as a student, as a teacher, as a colleague. And as the father of a daughter whose maturity and compassion I've never managed to match....

The rolling-out of all of these emotions, experiences, incidents and insights is imprinted like sharp-seriffed linotype on my being and my selfhood.

Trying to explain or even take charge of MY "self" in this *salmagundi* of existence is a needle-in-the-haystack kind of a thing ... and self-knowing, I know, is the hardest knowing of all.

MAORI culture names a deep wellspring of identity as *turangawaewae*: a "place to stand." But its geographic significance is found and established within the person.

Reaching beyond our Western concept of "home", it is the luxury of a landscape and natural harmony that shape inner relatedness ... that see one's "self" conformed with a place and all of its dimensions.

Turangawaewae confirms belonging and is felt as an assurance of inner strength. It's the bedrock of personal confidence, ease and security. And, because it is a place, it is a place to return to for restoration.

As an emigrant, a traveller and an irredeemable "foreigner" I'm denied that consolation. I live with the hunger. The closest I can come to it is the relationship I try to maintain with the ocean. Its horizons take me "home."

COLLECTIVELY, memories thrust themselves into our personalities, consciences and identities. We might call this "the voice of experience" but, of course, it runs deeper than that. Memory and experience color-in whatever we continue learning of life and help us to focus on what's around and before us.

It's more about what we notice than what is out there.

Although, whether we peer into shadows along a moonlit country road or the scattering of the same moonlight on a beach, or into the headlight streams of highway traffic, the play of our emotions will lead us away towards one place rather than another. Life's a wander through a lot of wayside distractions. In the same sort of way, our attitudes, values, expectations, experience, prejudices and preconceptions prod us toward some conclusions rather than others. Changing my mind's not as easy as I think.

> *Juan was cooking pieces of chicken on the outdoor barbecue. We talked, laughed and drank raw Brugal in the warm Dominican evening. Suddenly, from high above our heads there came a happy burst of trilling birdsong. Poised at the very top of a tall palm, its beak raised to a reddening sky, was a palmchat, the national bird of the Dominican Republic. Juan, who'd grown up in Santiago and hence in poverty, might have caviled about his situation and that of his country, but always had a story to share. The song of the Cigua Palmera (the palmchat's Spanish name) is a reminder of a tale, originally Costa Rican, about "La Segua": a beautiful young native-Spanish woman with pale skin, coal-black eyes and swishing long hair. Like the whole of Hispaniola, she was seized, raped and abandoned by an aristocratic Spanish administrator. Her spirit now lingers by remote pathways at night: an alluring phantom, ready to suddenly transform into a screaming, hideous ghoul and claw her grief and fury into the flesh of drunken and faithless lovers, male or female. As a warning against sexual predation,*

though, La Segua's hauntings have failed the Dominican Republic which too often sees needfulness and greed prostitute daughters of the poor to sleazy, rich, white tourists. So, the mythical Spanish Don also lives on, still the exploiter of youthful beauty. In the palm tree, the Segua fell silent; we had another rum. Chicken bones went on the fire.

I'VE LONG offered a workshop I call *With Love: Gifting Your Stories to Grandchildren*. I once had two sisters, Dutchwomen, take the course together. Three years apart, they'd experienced the German occupation of Holland during the Second World War.

Both remembered their neighbors smuggling scraps and peelings to a pig that lived in their basement. They planned to share and eat it clandestinely at Christmastime. One night, not long before Christmas, perhaps when they'd planned to kill the ill-fated animal, the pig escaped into the street. Despite a shoot-on-sight curfew and armed German soldiers, the family and their neighbors were soon silently, stealthily, stalking along the street after their Christmas dinner.

A floodlight suddenly lit the scene and a siren sent soldiers pouring into the street. There, blinking and bathed in light, stood the pig. A shot rang out and ricocheted off the cobblestones at its feet. The animal bolted and German soldiers, almost as hungrily as the local Dutch, charged after it. The girls and their neighbors followed. As I heard the story, the chase was joined by a crowd of hundreds.

The chaos of it all was remembered by the sisters as a wonderful taste of normality. At length there was a shot, a squeal, another shot and silence. There was a long stillness. Both sisters remembered the sudden silence, then the shouts of German troops as they herded the despondent Dutch back to their homes at bayonet-point. The pig was never seen again.

There are many ways of writing the story, but the two sisters had very different memories of it all. The younger one remembered the friendly piglet and identified it as a pet that was murdered by German soldiers ... then her shock after the war to be told that it had been intended to feed her family and their friends. The older sister best recalled the night of the chase and its excitement. She remembered that a German soldier had taken her hand and led her firmly home. "Bleiben sicher"—"be safe"—he had told her. It was a night that, for her, seemed to herald the end of the war and, perhaps, the end of her childhood.

Neither could remember the date.

OUR "real world" is a composite: a puzzle of innumerably entangled dimensions of countless sizes, meanings and dynamics. It is a maze of attractions and distractions, information and disinformation, motivations and experiences, each with its own secrets and its own destination, and it's always in motion. Moreover, this clamor exists within us, and we within it. It becomes the lens through which we see the present moment, and a bossy manager of our emotions.

Cornering any small part of all that's running free around us can become an imposition as inescapable as gravity. Depression will beget depression; uplift will bring uplift. Needfulness will generate needs. And fear? Fear.

Ordering memory into language helps to dissolve some of the chaos and find some measure of control. Words impose order and prime the assertiveness of a narrative: a story. And we need stories that give us strength, happiness, trustworthy values and well-grounded selfhood. This can mean wrenching ourselves away from security and familiarity to freshen our engagement with the whole of life. Or, more probably and less dangerously, to seek out nearby sources of beauty we've become blind to.

Still, we'll find, we are as bound by our culture as by our whimsy. Ways of telling are not entirely up to us. I'm baking bread as I write and it occurs to me that my memories are like the living, kneaded, buoyant dough. Stories are more like loaves of baked bread.

This is what cultures do. They teach us how to bake bread.

> *Imagine that I make a small clearing in the wilderness and plant a crop of food for the coming season. Or perhaps I drop a fish trap in the river. Pretty soon I'm setting conditions on others' access to the food that I'm collecting. That's despite my having staked it out from nature's indivisibility.*
>
> *Nor is it long until I start staking a claim to the food or resource as my own. I reinforce my fences, even if that limits others' access to what had been open commons. In no time at all, I've become less welcoming and less inclined to freely share.*
>
> *I soon find I have more than I need, and I start claiming privileges and asserting moral and cultural superiority in exchange for what I don't need. Sharing, once unthinking, becomes conditional. It gets seriously fraught when everybody wants to be like me but there's simply no more resource to go around. I innovate and squeeze a bit more out of what I can control and, when the "more" runs low, I get interested in taking from others, by guile or by force.*
>
> *I forget the commonality of what once was wild and feast myself as the creator of plenty. Rubbish piles up; I attract flies and my neighbors don't like me. So I don't like them. I can't think why. But I've run the full distance of my memory. I've forgotten that possession enslaves the possessor.*
>
> *Welcome to gravest problem facing the "West" in this 21st century.*

IN December, 2013, an industrial engineer called Heinz Puschmann died peacefully at his home in Auckland, New Zealand. During the Second World War, he had served with Hitler's elite 6th Fallschirmjager (Parachute) Regiment and been badly wounded in Normandy on D-Day. Several years after the war, he had moved to New Zealand.

"I always felt that what I was doing was right because I wasn't doing it for myself," he told war historian James Holland. "I was doing it for the Fatherland. I was protecting my home, my family, and many other families because it is my duty. I am not glorifying war, and please don't think I am ... war is terrible. It should be outlawed."[43]

In his book, *Casino to Trieste*, published in the year of his death, my dad wrote: "War is insanity personified. With the sophistication of modern weaponry, another war would destroy our whole world with all its wonders, its creatures great and small, its ocean and forests, its beautiful flowers and trees. We should be working as never before for peace, friendship and love."[44] He had gone to war with the conviction that Hitler had to be stopped. A former and future pacifist, he was drafted into the New Zealand Army in 1941. He rose through the ranks to become an infantry captain, was wounded and won the Military Cross. "My personal philosophy was simple: The better soldier I am, the sooner we'll all go home."

My dad and Heinz Puschmann, fellow engineers, would meet years later and become mutually respectful friends. They discovered that back in March 1944, during the Third Battle of Cassino, they had been determinedly trying to kill each other. Both had memories of heavy rains, constant shelling, laying antipersonnel mines and making do in stone ruins reeking of death and ordure ... holding their ground. "It was horrendous," Heinz Puschmann told James Holland. "We were fighting against the New Zealanders. With many veteran troops from North Africa and Crete, the New Zealanders were among the most tenacious and experienced troops the Allies had."

More than 60 million people are reckoned to have died in that war.

That was all a long time ago. But there was an awful lot of blood.

> *Everybody runs in city rain*
> *as if the claustrophobia's*
> *made suddenly stark-clear*
> *and suddenly something's to fear*
> *... slapped aside by windscreen wipers,*
> *hissed from the angry tires,*
> *but cleaving in return*
> *newsprint's sodden tidings*
> *like omens to the sidewalk ...*
> *Everybody runs in the city rain*
> *as if it might sweep them away ...*
> *but nobody smiles at the thought.*
> *Dark patterns stutter across the grey asphalt*
> *and chuckle on the window-panes,*
> *drumming and strumming ...*
> *crystal babble in the crevices,*

drifting mists across the empty park:
cold fingers reach down cringing necks
socks wettened to discomfort ...
slicking hair to forward-frowning skulls
and the city sees its garments
wettened to transparency ...
Everybody runs in the city rain as if ...
As if the umbrellas dripping in elevators
might somehow muddle or subdue
the tyrannies of artificial light ...
or loosen civility's delicate chains.
Yes, everybody runs in the city rain ...

STILL the wars grind on. Small, cruel, hateful ones are the in-thing. They seem almost normal. They seem almost moral.

The global situation nowadays surpasses the dissolute last days of the Roman or British Empires: troublesome, never-to-be-resolved border conflicts and rebellions ... refugees, child soldiers, guerrilla fighters, corruption and civilian casualties, "terrorists," "improvised explosive devices," suicide bombers, kidnappings and hostage-takings, militias, extremists, insurgents, extortion, ambushes, propaganda, direct or indirect insurrection. But no ruler wants rival powers barging in and taking over, regardless of any benefit they may offer. So they pull others' strings, provide munitions and propagandize. There are profit-taking opportunities at almost every level. Rising liabilities are clung to along with remembered assets.

Perversely one may think, given the shock devastations wrought on Hiroshima and Nagasaki, the United States and Russia have reportedly stockpiled more than 7,000 nuclear warheads, souvenirs of their Cold War heydays. Considerably fewer are held by Britain, France, China, Pakistan, Israel, India and North Korea. So there are ample munitions to turn the world to sterile toast many times over. The numbers are so large as to be incomprehensible. But it's the scope of suffering that should worry us.

American military spending is astronomical: three times that of China, seven times that of Russia, $640 billion in 2014. Wikipedia observes that, in addition, the United States was spending at least $179 billion in the period 2010–2018 on its nuclear arsenal, averaging $20 billion per year. Despite recent President Barack Obama's attempts in the media to reduce the scope of the current nuclear arms race, the U.S. plans to spend a further $1 trillion over the next 30 years to modernize its nuclear arsenal. According to Wikipedia, the United States and its close allies are responsible for two-thirds to three-quarters of the world's military spending.

In what sense is this "defence"?

HEART disease and cancer have become the leading causes of death in the U.S. Both are widely related to lifestyle and diet. After that, it's accidents, mostly car smashes. Poisoning became the leading cause of injury death in the United States in 2014. And the American suicide rate in 2014 climbed: to 13 per 100,000 people ... 20.7 for males, and most especially among men aged 75 and over. Yet people in the richest countries seem to be the most fearful of death.

OUR brains' perceptual processes don't like gaps. They darn the holes and stitch the edges together. They use insight, assumption, emotion, information, misconception and illusion.

At a deeper level, our culturally and perceptually fabricated "self"—and its juggling of reason, emotion and idle preference—can ignite passionate motivations that seem crazy or baseless to an onlooker. A casual onlooker will see action without a cause: the seer's artless chuckle, the hero's selfless daring, the miser's reflexive greed or the bigot's crazy rage.

I've just been sitting out in my shorts and a tee in the rain: a light, ineffective rain. But rain, nonetheless, and I love rain. After 20 minutes, I'm cooled but hardly soaked through. I was rekindling memories—some fresh and clear, some on the edges of non-recall. No reason. Memories hold me like elastic tethers, like the rain. But ephemerality gives me emotional hiccups. The mix has my awareness dancing in the air, frustrating the traction I need to enter panoramas of new experience—like sitting reflectively in the rain—that could free me. Spectres of the unfamiliar, of suspicions, of skewed perceptions do us no favors. Childhood norms linger in our memories. In looking forward, my view is prescribed. I dangle in a universe of possibilities that's far from infinite. My options are choices, not chance as I might hope, despite having always sought the unfamiliar. To fly, I have to tension what most strongly holds and restrains me, and let that propel me into tomorrows I cannot imagine.

AND there are experiences that aren't what they seem to be. They are illusions.

A Fata Morgana is one of the less common and most complicated of mirages.

"Fata Morgana" is the Italian name for the Arthurian sorceress Morgan le Fay, from a belief that these mirages, often seen in the Strait of Messina, were fairy castles in the air, or illusory lands created by her witchcraft to draw sailors to their deaths.

Fata Morgana mirages are seen as narrow bands right above the horizon. They form when light is bent as it passes through a steep "thermal inversion" where a layer of warm air overlays a layer markedly cooler air. And, in calm weather, the layers of cooler and warmer air can act like a refracting lens, bending the light and creating a series of images.

Images of the real objects that are their sources get distorted beyond recognition and stacked upside-down and right-side-up—some stretched, others compressed—on top of each other. And the effect can change quite quickly.

Like other mirages, the Fata Morgana is a real, physical effect. The air, which we don't see, acts as a lens that shapes what we do see. And, if it distorts what we see, it can contribute to some bad outcomes.

Mirages like this have led navigators astray at sea, and sent lost travellers to their deaths in deserts and in the Arctic. It's been suggested that the *Titanic* disaster was possibly caused and probably worsened by atmospheric anomalies of the sort.

And mirages have their parallels in the functioning of cultures and societies, our own included.

> I'M dreaming now. I will remember drifting in a shifting formlessness, a colorful ether I can explore freely in three dimensions, an abstraction maybe from my diving days. Moving about, I find myself in webs of interconnections where, behind one remembered experience or person, I find more and more increasingly abstract but increasingly interlinked images. It's all very surreal ... and an often encountered figure is that of a boy who looks about eight or ten years old. He's been in my dreams for 30 years. He has a blue balloon on a string. He begins to eat it; it doesn't burst, it's like eating an apple. For some years now, he has begun sharing it with me.
> The air within tastes pear-like, and has a little of that grittiness of pear flesh. Other familiar presences are a mako shark and a duck, both of them friendly, reassuring.
> There's seldom a singular, clear narrative line ... but birds and beaches often appear and become people; friends. And I become me.

THERE is an extreme, unprecedented glut of entertainment these days; it's even portable. Streaming video, YouTube, cable channels, Netflix and the like ... close to 30,000 podcasts: the choice itself offers addicts a 24-7 psychic invasion.

Please don't tell me that this is what shapes selfhood these days.

It's too easy to forget that just three or four generations ago, music was mostly home-made. Families sang songs together around a piano or played an instrument. None of it was amplified. Travelling theatre ensembles might sometimes visit and, in summer, a circus might come to a nearby town. Community drama clubs, bands, choirs, amateur theatricals and church suppers were standard social attractions. Books, then radio filled evenings at home. And, in general terms, the society that bore us was hierarchical, unjust, warlike, smug, bigoted, brutal and, far too often, recklessly stupid.

Growing up in New Zealand, I was already at university when my parents bought their first black and white television ... and I was too busy to ever watch it. Besides, I had a job in a late-night coffee bar where a live jazz trio played till "all hours," cigarette smoke filled the air and there were weekend floor shows for which I worked the lights. We were night people and had our own social life. Nights "off" were party nights. As often as not, I got to spend my daytime alone or with friends in the ocean: diving and spearfishing, swimming, surfing and sometimes sailing as a stand-in crew member. Or caving, or hiking in the bush. Everything seemed accessible, energy seemed limitless and opportunities all entailed choices. All of it was all "real" risk-carrying experience. So it took me rather a long time to finish a Bachelor of Arts degree. Then I went into fulltime journalism with a big morning daily which meant shifts from two in the afternoon to eleven at night and new circles of camaraderie. I met politicians, celebrities, criminals, Olympic gold medalists, entertainers, scientists, cops, chancers and business magnates. It was fun; every day was a parade. I was finding it harder to spend time with "ordinary" people.

Since then, experience has further contracted. Electronic media offer choices from vast arrays of new, edited or simulated, unrealities. "Connectivity" has risen at the cost of intimacy. For many people, busy-ness has shifted from hurrying from one place to the next on time (local clock time) to role-juggling in virtual time.

And my dreams have become mostly abstract, interesting and often inexplicable. I've sometimes woken urgently in the middle of the night with fresh ideas or insights I can't express; I've laughed loudly enough to wake myself — and my wife. But I'm a "night person" given to sleeping in. So, more often, more simply, and more reluctantly, I'll wake in the morning feeling at emotional ease. I can't remember having had a nightmare since I was at boarding school a long, long, alien time ago. And I don't remember any of them.

MOST dreams are forgotten, but dreams and visions have widely entered religious thought and cultural practice. I suspect they help to shape us too.

Australian aboriginal peoples shared their dreams every morning and planned their days around them. Early Mesopotamians and ancient Egyptians kept written records of them. Some cultures have voracious appetites for dreams, reaching for them through self-inflicted physical stresses or drugs. Some cultures receive them simply as gifts from the "gods". Many have seen them as peeks into the future.

Startling dreams played a big part in early Hebrew scripture and most of the big events in the Bible are pre-figured by dreams: Jacob and his ladder, Joseph and his standing sheaves of grain; Pharaoh's vision of famine; the dream of Jesus' innocence that frightened Pilate's wife ... and John of Patmos' apocalyptic vision, described in his Revelation. Islam, too, has a deep respect for, and interest in, dreams.

A lesser dream gave the inventor of the sewing machine, Elias Howe, the crucial idea of threading needles near their point. Abraham Lincoln dreamt a premonition of his assassination, Robert Louis Stevenson dreamed the plot of *Dr. Jekyll and Mr. Hyde*, and it was a dream that gave James Watson the double helix image which explained the structure of the DNA molecule.

Nor let us forget Lady Macbeth and her dream-led ilk.

Sigmund Freud erected his psychiatric theories on the sands of his patients' dreams. He located dreams in the "subconscious" and understood them as expressions of hidden feelings and appetites. Carl Jung preferred to see them as paths to emotional and spiritual healing. Fritz Perls extended Jung's approach, and pioneered Gestalt psychotherapy with its focus on the depths of the present moment. He'd hoped to set up a community in Canada on Vancouver Island. His death saw it instead founded by the Toronto psychiatrist Harvey Freedman and his colleague Jorge Rosner as the Gestalt Institute of Toronto.

Its tenor was along the lines of what's been called *The Gestalt Prayer*:

> *I do my thing and you do your thing. I am not in this world to live up to your expectations, and you are not in this world to live up to mine.*
> *You are you, and I am I, and if by chance we find each other, it's beautiful. If not, it can't be helped.*[45]

EVERYBODY dreams. But, despite their universality and the influences that dreams have had on our cultures, dream content has attracted less academic research than you might expect.

Instead, we know that dreams happen during a particular period of semi-consciousness called REM (rapid eye movement) sleep because, during it, our eyes flick around as though watching a busy crowd. But, despite all of the activity, it seems to be the most important sort of sleep—the kind that when, deprived of it, we feel most uncomfortable. Some researchers see this dream-sleep as a kind of housekeeping phase, its content having no particular meaning or value.

Dr. Ernest Hartmann is interested in the way that the dream state triggers widespread activity in the brain. Rather than simply structuring a memory, he sees this process "smoothing things out" and harmonizing memories with their contexts and, for the longer term, making wider connections. Dr. Hartmann is professor of psychiatry at the Tufts University School of Medicine and director of the Sleep Disorders Center at Newton-Wellesley Hospital in Newton, Massachusetts,

Dreams, he believes, help us to "level off" in a safe place, whether or not the dreams are actually remembered.

A remembered dream, he suggests, may play a role in problem solving, science, art, and self-knowledge ... a search, perhaps, for ground on which to stand?

"LEVELING off in a safe place" seems a bit at odds with some of the things dreams have inspired me to do. Dreams have nudged me—and others I know—into a bit of risk-taking here and there.

Youth, more than reality it seems, stirred dreams that persuaded me I was indestructible and encouraged episodes of recklessness that leveler—"older and wiser"—heads would never have entertained.

So where do the dreams come from? Hormones? And where did those influences come from? And, inevitably, who is the "me" that makes a response?

Oh, if only it were possible, "self knowledge" would be a wonderful thing. Or is "self" all that we know....

All that we can ever know?

If we knew that ... heavens, that could really be something.

6
It's All Just Stories

TRENT RIVER-RICE LAKE, ONTARIO, CANADA

LIKE the silvery glints of a fish struggling upstream, against the flow and the probabilities of its passage, meaning is something we glimpse in the flows of a real world that clatters and rumbles along on its unstoppable way. We construct meaning, rather the way we discern the fish ... at first in our imaginations. We shape it out of our hopes, memories, fears, expectations and our creative impulse—all of that. It becomes a vivid image long before it takes our bait, is reeled in and lies flopping at our feet. Sometimes it's not a fish at all. We've been mistaken.

Although, whether we peer into shadows along a moonlit country road or the scattering of the same moonlight on a beach, or into the headlight streams of highway traffic, the play of our emotions will lead us away towards one place rather than another. Life's a wander through a lot of wayside distractions. In the same sort of way, our attitudes, values, expectations, experience, prejudices and preconceptions prod us toward some conclusions rather than others. Changing my mind's not as easy as I think.

We may find we've colored-in our world before we see it up close or in daylight, by which time rough guesses and first impressions can have hardened into convictions. So we say in our defence: it's "better to be safe than sorry," "better the devil you know" and "better be on the safe side" because "leopards never change their spots," "apples fall close to the tree," "a bird in the hand is worth two in the bush" and "curiosity killed the cat." And there always used to be "more fish in the sea" anyway. So "don't rock the boat": it's easier to be "wise after the event."

But yes, we are born with the wonderful, magical power of finding traceries of meaning, order and uniqueness in the rush of events that carry us along. We find meaning and, having found it, can feel empowered to shape new places to live and new ways of living in company with other people. Our dread of the chaos falls from us, we give ourselves the power to act, analyze, and shape destinies we'll believe are of our own making ... and, at the root of it all, is our sense of story.

Intuitively, we compose and tell stories all the time. They come in all sorts of forms: a mathematical proof's a "story," and so is a chemical equation: both are abstract accounts of experience, a portable glimmer of insight. A musical score, an architect's plan, an accounting ledger, a flower arrangement—these are "stories" too.

In a story, everything leads to something or to somewhere new and, therefore, towards hope or despair. Everything has its own story. My favorite cotton shirt was made in China, the world's biggest grower, user and importer of cotton. In some parts of the world, cotton is still picked by hand. Think of the travels a coin in your pocket might have had, if only you knew. Think of the other minds and lives that have been influenced by a book you've read or a place you've been. Let life stretch your cultural boundaries through its narratives.

Story is the up-front, explicit stuff that fuels our performing, oral and literary arts, all the way back to their origins. And stories are the essential stuff of daily conversation, whether it's the quick sharing of a bit of gossip, the thoughtful telling of our hopes, or the description of some activity we're engaged in. Stories run this way and that through everything we say and feel about all we experience, then nestle into our memory.

> *In one of the bygone chapters of our life, we kept a house-cow: a gentle, pretty, friendly thing who'd follow us around. A good friend was staying with us and, at milking time, said she'd like to bring our cow to the barn. Time passed and we began to wonder what was taking so long ... and then we saw them. Far up the hill, our friend was trying to drive our cow ahead of her. And our cow was trying to follow. Our friend went behind the cow and waved her arms. Our cow turned to face and follow her. At this, our friend went behind our cow again and, again, the cow turned to face her. Both were ever more deeply confusing each other. "Just come!" we called, and they came down the hill together.*

SHARED stories prime relationships, build communities and define cultures. Heard, a story enters the world of our conscious experience and changes, perhaps in just a small way, the way we appreciate and think about the world at large—and this, in turn, changes us. We act a little differently and are responded to a little differently. And so we are shaped by the stories we've heard and created. We enjoy moving among people who've heard stories that are familiar to us. In such ways, some stories shape nations. Others bring them down.

There are stories we "just don't want to hear." After all, a story can harm us as devastatingly as a physical assault; some stories nudge us to new appetites for joy. A story can carry insights into all sorts of experiences but, in its telling, a story is usually about a particular occurrence.

A group of people, a principle, a historical incident, a place or a motivation can be given clarity by personifying it as a character. I suspect this is how people came to talk about gods ... or, more conveniently, about *a* god: it is a way of giving experience a common grounding, shape and context. In that structured form, the narrative can widen insight and deepen creativity.

A story leads from one place, time or condition to another. It keeps things simple and accessible, leaving out incidentals if favor of a consistent core logic. As well, a story usually has "closure," leaving no questions hanging, unless deliberately; it has a consistent point of view and "voice." A story that leaves essential questions carelessly open, won't "ring true."

A successful story is self-contained; it stands apart from the broad flow of history: a device to rekindle past experience in a new present. (This is especially true, and effective, in oral cultures, and in oral performance where a resurrected "present" can be deeply, keenly and immediately felt.)

Old stories can characterize or give context to new events. So someone can "cross the Rubicon" (or the "Delaware") and "meet their Waterloo." A "Judas" can destroy a "Romeo." We have "Catch 22s," "Holy Grails," "Herculean tasks" and "Hobson's choices" ... even if we don't exactly remember the stories that seeded them.

> *In my days as a daily newspaper reporter, it sometimes bothered me that the stories I wrote, though balanced, "accurate" and all the rest of it, betrayed the reality they set out to convey. For one thing, by the time the story reached its reader, the real world had moved on; the people it referred to had gone on to other things, and the consequences of whatever had taken place had been swept away towards resolutions of their own. A news story is too succinct a narrative to describe the precursors of an event. Yet this is the very information that would make "news" intelligible to the people reading it. The news story was never the "real story" ... nor could it be.*
>
> *Moreover, we were trained to write in a "pyramid" form, starting with an "intro" that, in as few words as possible, told the who, the what, the where and the when. The "how" and "why" were to follow in descending levels of significance. This let a subeditor cut*

the story from the bottom to fit the available space, without much harm being done. I learned to write to length, and to gauge the butterfly-like attention span of "the reader." Research has shown that few news stories are read or heard past the second or third paragraph. Many are understood only in as much as they confirm a reader's existing biases. Now, I've come to the realization that ALL stories can have similar shortcomings.

As propagandists know all too well, stories owe their power to their emotional jolt as well as—or, sometimes, instead of—any factual content. They need to be "true" in the way they resonate or conflict with their hearer's experience. And they reach other people when they engage their hearer's hopes, memories, fears, expectations and creative impulses. They can arouse vivid images long before anything "real" is exposed to us.

That glint in the water? It may not have been a fish at all.

It's worth reflecting on the implications of the fact that, having once heard a story, you can never "un-hear" it. Hence the tenacity of prejudices, biases and misplaced loyalties that, in the darker corners of complicated modern societies, endure generation to generation.

It all comes down to "meaning." Information that stands too apart from a governing narrative is mostly seen as cognitive litter. If we can't find a useful place to put it, we'll discard it altogether.

To all intents and purposes, information's infinite. To be "real," information has to be sieved, selected and organized into patterns that can be compacted and securely lodged in a story—or a theory (a story in an academic gown): a story that's tidy enough to nudge its way into our limited, habit-sustained and already crammed human minds. It has to be "believable" in the sense of being conceivable and meshing with the other narratives in our heads. Then, from little stories, bigger tales can be crafted, and bigger ones again until we have an entire culture, a world.

> *I have a lovely book called* Birds of My Kalam Country *by an anthropologist, the late Ralph Bulmer, and Ian Saem Majnep, a Kalam native New Guinea Highlander from the Kaironk Valley. The book is an outline of the Kalam classification system—a "taxonomy"—for the birds that inhabit the Kaironk Valley. They are an intimate part of the lives of these people—as a food source, yes, but also in dreams, wisdom tradition and ritual. And the classification system incorporates all of this so that it amounts to an outline of the birds' habits and habitat, their forms and colors, and of their uses and relationships with people. It is very different from both the Latin-using, physiology-based taxonomic system of the eighteenth-century Swedish biologist Carolus Linnaeus that prevailed in the 1960s when this book was written and the new*

genomes-based "cladistic" system. But it's only the Kalam system that would help you to survive in the Kaironk Valley.

EVERY story, heard, told and remembered, brings us face to face with tantalizing and dangerously vital questions about "truth." Here's a story a history teacher once told me. I doubt its factual truth and I can't remember which of my history teachers told it. I have only vague recollections of most of them. But I do remember the story.

> *It was during the English Civil War, 1642–51. July: Two squadrons of Royalist cavalry were moving north. A foraging troop returned to the main body of mounted soldiers having seen a smaller detachment of Parliamentarian infantry marching south towards them.*
> *The Royalist major decided to annihilate the slow-moving foot soldiers. It was clear that, preferring flatter ground, they'd follow the low road between two ranges of low hills. So, he posted lookouts and led one squadron to a patch of woods at the far end of the valley. He then sent his second-in-command, a captain noted for his courage, with the second squadron to wait in ambush behind the lower easterly range.*
> *The plan was that, when the infantrymen approached the woods, the major would lead a frontal attack. Once they engaged, the captain would lead an attack on their flank and, together, they would wipe the encircled Parliamentarian troops out.*
> *It was a hot day.*
> *The captain led his squadron off to the right and over farmland to an old Roman road that cut a straight path, out of sight of the valley, to a crossroads. There was a pub, and a field where local people obviously held their market days. The squadron rode into the field, dismounted and let their horses drink from the troughs. The troopers took off their hot helmets and settled down in the sun to wait for the signal to attack.*
> *It was a hot day. The cavalrymen's eyes, then their thoughts were drawn past their refreshed horses, to the pub. The pub keeper, seeing the soldiers, opened the door and waited.*
> *A young recruit, unable to contain his longings, asked his cornet if maybe they could go for a drink, just one, a small one, while they waited, and get out of the sun. "Silence," the young cornet barked. But other soldiers had been thinking the same thing. "Come on, sir," asked an old hero. "You could at least ask the lieutenant." Other troopers joined the call.*
> *So the cornet asked the lieutenant. The lieutenant was a drinking*

man and, when cornets from two of the other squad sought the same permission, he went to ask the squadron captain. The captain had bought his commission and was a little inexperienced, but he could see his soldiers' growing discontent. And he liked the battle-hardened lieutenant who'd advised him well in the past.

It was a hot day.

One drink might raise the men's spirits and stiffen their will, thought the captain. He called the two lieutenants over and told them to let their men have a pint apiece on their own account, then to re-form back in the field. When the word reached the men they cheered their captain, the major, the King and their cause.

Meanwhile, the company of Parliamentarian infantry had entered the valley unawares and was plodding on towards the woods: the cool, shady, beckoning woods, where they could rest secure.

It was a hot day.

As the cornets soon discovered, and the captain and his lieutenants feared, a dry dragoon is not easily halted at a single pint. The ale hit the spot with the captain too, so he had a second as a privilege of his rank. But the lieutenants and the cornets were as dry and sweated-out as their men; what harm could a second pint possibly do? So, as they invariably do, one thing led to another....

It was a hot day and, when a company of Royalist cavalry came dashing at them from the wood they were so keen to reach, the foot soldiers formed up, loaded their muskets with an especially bitter personal anger and deadly resolve. The major rode hard in front, brandishing his sword and spurring his horse forward. The first volley felled him. The second volley cut down a score of his men and heartened the infantrymen who presented their pikes and stood firm.

The lookouts from the ridge galloped down to the market field where they could see their comrades' horses gathered. "Quick," they cried, "where is the captain?" Pressing through the laughing, merry throng in the pub, they had pints of ale pressed into their hands and their heads were buzzing by the time they found the group of drinking officers. There were by now bottles of port on the table and troopers were singing bawdy barrack room songs. A passing milkmaid knew better than to look in, and hurried on down the road.

To cut a long story somewhat short, the steady infantrymen decimated the over-confident cavalry company. After piking, dirking and slashing the wounded, horseless troopers and officers to death, they rested in the woods and drank from a stream that ran through the shade. A passing milkmaid told one of their sentries about the scene at the pub. So, with their swords, dirks and pikes

already bloodied, the infantrymen set off over the ridge.
It was a cool evening, and as the stars began to shine, the weary foot soldiers expended the last of their strength stabbing and hacking every last drunk or snoring cavalryman to death, including the cornets, the lieutenants and the captain. Then they hanged the pub keeper from the tree and emptied his last stocks of ale to celebrate their victory.
Now, because the two, now lost, squadrons of cavalry might well have turned the tide in a battle or two, and even the war, this little known incident raises historical questions. Firstly, who's to blame for the beheading of King Charles, a few years later? Who was to blame for the debacle in the valley and at the crossroads?
Was it the major who, after all, didn't know about the pub and whose plan was really rather good? Was it the captain who intended only to fire his men's battle spirit? Was it the young dragoon who first uttered the words that were on so many minds? Was it the tale-telling milkmaid? Maybe it was the pub keeper, now swinging by his neck from the tree at his door? Or could his predecessor who'd built the pub be culpable? But, let's be reasonable, the crossroads brought the market days, and the market days called for a pub. Was it the Roman engineers who built the roads? Was it the Parliamentarians who fought so desperately, so ruthlessly? What was the battle all about? Where was there any virtue? Was it the King himself? Or Cromwell?
Or can it all be blamed on a hot day in July? War itself can be like that.

TRACING the passage of raw experience, all the way through our consciousness to the stories that seed and give it memorable form, would help us to know ourselves much better than we do. But that sort of introspection would stall the brisk efficiency of our workaday social relationships.

The impulses at work in that transformation are the workings of a tapestry weaver: adeptly passing the thread-bound bobbins back and forth within the confines of the loom's frame. A design's conceived and rendered, and emerges in a very different medium, free but particular, and recognizable to different people in different ways. But the threads that cross and contrast, take form in planes that are supple, textured and weighted around the shoulders of forms yet to appear ... and the weaving of them becomes a practiced task, a medley of integrated physiological habits. And, despite the weaver's meticulous craft, the finished weaving's always enmeshed in surprise.

A story's always like that too: gathering meaning as ideas and experiences are brought together, warp and weft, and enmeshed in the capacity to surprise even its creator.

STORIES exist in time and are made of air ... of words and ideas.

When I hear the word "fish," the image that swims to mind is quite specific: it's a New Zealand schnapper*— its glistening, pale-purplish upper parts and silvery-white belly, the iridescent blue dots, the deep body and pointed face, the scales that stuck to my hands: the prize catch of every hungry fisherman, and they were plentiful in those days of my youth.

With all of that, come recollected smells, sights and sensations: salt on my skin, tide-lapped wharf piles, green string fishing lines wound on sticks, hooks and lead sinkers, pieces of yellowtail bait washed this way and that by bilge water in rocking, clinker-built white dinghies, sunburn and expanses of sea. I think of those times when my dad got home early from work and we'd go and catch a schnapper or two for dinner. We had to scale and clean them of their purplish and grey-white entrails because my mother didn't like "fish guts" in the kitchen. We'd do that at the beach with seagulls mobbing us to make off with the scraps. Only later did I learn to gut, fillet and skin with one fairly smooth movement of a knife, running it from a cut behind the head, down the spine of the fish to the tail, then flipping the fillet and continuing the knife stroke under the flesh to lift it from the skin: once for each side. Fresh from the sea, schnapper (like most sea fish) is delicious raw and we sometimes filleted and ate one before we headed home.

> *It was 1959. I was 13 years old. The loathsome Anglican boarding school in which I was by then languishing decided it would be a "good thing" to send its juniors off to hear the famous American evangelist Billy Graham strut his stuff. He was making a highly publicized tour of New Zealand with his circus, performing in Auckland at the big international rugby park. I hated crowds, having got caught up in one a few years previously. Moths drifted through the floodlights' glare and the stands were packed. Spotlights flared and swung onto a song and dance warm-up by his touring entourage of shiny-eyed devotees. Then the great man himself took the stage and began pumping up the worst end of my bad attitudes' repertoire. I'd seen those black-and-white newsreels of Nazi rallies and I started drawing conclusions that they and my father's Second World War narratives had instilled. In the whipped-up, crowd-chorused "amen's," I sourly heard the sonic and emotional profiles of the "Sieg heil's" of the 1930s. This "god" was an Albtraum.† "His" idea of "love" was to let a few flatterers escape the eternal torture that "He" had devised for creatures "He" claimed to have created. That, at least was the impression forming in my mind as more vulnerable members of the crowd began fainting from emotional overload. I recoiled. On the bus back to school,*

---

* Now often spelled "snapper": *Pagrosomus auratus,* sometimes called a "silver sea bream."
† *Albtraum* (German): a nightmare.

I declared that I was an atheist. I knew the word, but not really what it meant. It was a rash move: the intensified bullying would persuade me that Christians and Nazis were cut from the same cloth. I began reading all I could get my hands on about atheism: Schopenhauer, Marx, Comte, Sartre, Feuerbach ... positivism, pragmatism, materialism, existentialism, whatever was proffered at the progressive bookstores in town. Okay, I failed to understand much of it, and failed horribly and naively to make any connection between the rhetoric I was reading and Aryan fascism. I was still forming a vocabulary and happy to let it part ways with most of my peers at school. To "god" I gave particularly ugly overtones. And Billy Graham? I still sometimes tell people that he "converted" me. He did.

THERE are scholarly debates about how we originally got into language.

Spoken or written, words have countless ways of touching us at different levels, and of interacting with each other to heighten effect, memorability and meaning. As "tools" go, they can be blunt and punchy or subtle and remarkably precise.

It's been demonstrated that, while an emotion can bring a word to mind and into our conversations, a word can stir an emotion to life by giving it a name.

The Japanese word *amae*, for example, identifies a reassuring feeling of confidence that others will offer you their support when you need it. *Frühjahrsmüdigkeit* is probably too much of a mouthful to export but in German it neatly fills the need for a way to identify that low, grey sense of despond that accompanies the start of a low-lit northern winter day.

Dictionaries give us standard definitions of words based on the way they've been used, and offer tips about a word's pronunciation, origins and standard spelling. But they take time to compile, so they lag behind living usage. Spoken language is looser and livelier, buffeted into shape by day-to-day interactions between people in conversation.

Words and languages are living, fluid things, and ours to explore and play with to convey, not just information, but also emotions, attitudes, values and culture.

So, while there are dictionary meanings, they are, at best, the bare bones. The *Oxford Dictionary* definition of the word *dog*, for example, goes something like: "A domesticated carnivorous mammal that typically has a long snout, an acute sense of smell, non-retractile claws, and a barking, howling, or whining voice." I don't know about you but when I reach out and pat our old collie-shepherd cross, or take her walking, the dictionary's description of her is worlds apart from what's running through my mind.

Emotion's inseparable from words, all words. A way to get a sense of this is to play with a simplified version of something psychologists call a "semantic differential." Developed by the psychologist Charles E. Osgood to explore meaning, it invites people to rate a word's "meaning" by positioning it between pairs of opposed adjectives. It's found a number of uses but it doesn't explain meaning. Rather it draws out attitudes and emotional profiles. And it's rare to find two people who agree very far down the list.

Try it for yourself. Just make a list of, say, 20 pairs of opposed adjectives: hot-cold, rough-smooth, big-little, hard-soft, wet-dry, long-short, fast-slow, dark-light, attractive-repugnant, strong-weak, loud-quiet, happy-sad, dirty-clean, near-far, tough-fragile, passive-active, good-bad, sweet-sour, heavy-light, crooked-straight, familiar-strange... things like that.

Next: take a word, any word. A noun is best. Write it down then, quickly and associating freely, decide which adjective of each pair better suits whatever's named by the word. Is it more "hot" or more "cold"? More "rough" or more "smooth"? And so on. Make a record of your responses.

Now, persuade someone else to try the same exercise with the same word and record their choices. You'll find points of agreement, but you'll also discover you're at odds on some characteristics and, if you talk about those differences, you'll often find reasonable reasons for seeing things differently. Knowing this, the police get suspicious if witness statements are too similar.

In fact, of course, we each have our own deeper, fine-tuned understandings of each word in our vocabulary. And, if you worry at it too hard, you might wonder that we're able to communicate at all. The way we understand and respond to words is grounded in our experiences, and we communicate most readily within families, communities or subcultures where the bounds of experience are similar.

Cross-culturally, communication gets altogether fraught. Time, nature and even the human body are understood and interacted with in deeply different ways in different cultures and, although words can be found to identify objects and actions in common, their significance and the emotions they call up can be very different.

> *NEW ZEALAND: I was the editor of a rural local newspaper and had stopped to talk with a farmer standing at his gate waiting for the herd tester. We got talking about the way the region had become some of the country's most productive land since a cobalt deficiency had been diagnosed and corrected by topdressing.*
> *"Yeah, I'm bloody lucky, I really am," the farmer told me. "I've got the sweetest farm around here. It was on the small side when dad was a kid but since the cobalt thing, it's just the right size for me to run and it's not too bad a living." We talked on. "Actually, when you think about it, this land all around here, it really is the best land in the Waikato," he said.*
> *Then, after a smoke: "Of course, the Waikato's New Zealand's prime agricultural area, way best, for sure. The country'd be up shit creek without it." The talk shifted to exports. "I reckon New Zealand's got it all sewn up, with the horticulture now and*

all ... we'd have to be the best farming country in the world. Yeah, it's the climate, I know, and the land. But we've got the right approach here too. I pity the poor bloody Aussies when I think about it."

I suddenly realized I was talking to the world's best farmer who happened to have the best farm in the world.

WORDS are colored by their sound. Sounds can be very evocative. They often underlie slang usages and probably account for many of those "origins obscure" entries in the dictionaries. They're exploited in the naming of brands and products by advertisers and by political propagandists. Again, they can be very misleading across cultures.

To an English speaker's ear, for example, the sound of *kønne piger* doesn't seem immediately attractive. It's Danish for "pretty girls." In Norwegian, you'd say *vakker jente*. The Danish word *hygge* has no one-word English equivalent: it carries a meaning something like "bliss" or "happy tranquility": the soothing contentment of all things being well.

In Hawkes Bay, New Zealand, there's a pretty river and its name, Tutaekuri (which sounds like "too-tye-coo-ree"), sounds apt enough to an English speaker's ear, evocative of clear water tumbling over sun-kissed, round-worn boulders towards the sea. But the name translates to mean the stuff that dogs drop on neighbors' lawns that you then step in, carry indoors on your shoes and grind into the carpet, all the time wondering where the dreadful smell is coming from. "Shit Creek" would be a fair translation. But the river's name refers more directly to the dog's entrails than their contents, the riverbank having once been a place where butchered dogs were cleaned and prepared for cooking. The idea of tucking in on dog meat offends a lot of Westerners. It was essential protein to many Polynesians.

Even nonsense words have allusion-stirring sounds. So it's possible to tell an English nonsense word from a Chinese or Spanish nonsense word. Real words run a real risk of being misheard, so the intentions behind can be misunderstood.

THE rhymes and rhythms that words set up can make a passage of speech more memorable, or turn it into a rap. In print, a word's look can influence the way it's responded to. Some letters are rotund and curvaceous, others stark. Based on shapes alone, it's possible to get an emotional reading of sorts: *k, w, t, j, v, y, l, i, z, x* and *q* have sharp corners and bits that stick up and down. They have a "feel" to them that's different the round, smooth letters like *o, m, n, u, a, c,* s *n* and *e*. So we have a difference in appearance as well as sound between say *case, trunk* and *valise; collide* and *impact; warp* and *bend; pith* and *core; green* and *sour; smell* and *stink*, and so on. And the typographic appearance of the first few words of a passage can help to nudge the reader's expectations this way or that.

It's Just Stories

FINALLY, every word has a history. A language is a living, changing, dynamic thing and there's no stopping it. There are reckoned to be rather more than 300 million people around the world who speak English as their first language and they all use English more or less differently: differently from people in other parts of the world, differently from their neighbors and differently even from their parents. They're all adding new words to the language and dropping old words. They're bending usages and coining new usages. You can't stop them and you certainly can't hold a living language in a state of suspended animation. Change is guaranteed.

Most of the words in English right now never bother us because they have rarefied technical or regional uses. A medium-sized, modern dictionary has about 100,000 entries, but Shakespeare got by knowing about 30,000—which is probably around the number of words you and I know.

Some words leap into power and significance because of what they identify in the present: a person of particular status, a place that's vividly colored by history, or an iconic object. Others lose their usefulness as society moves on. They drop from use and collective memory. Yet others merge into new meanings.

Each word has a life of its own and its own story. Once upon a time, for example, in the language that linguists identify as "Indo-European," there was a word *wen*, meaning desire or love. It was a word that gave the Roman goddess of love and beauty her name: *Venus*—an object of desire, of pursuit. But the goddess' name was just one of a number of words to incorporate roots like *uen, wan, win, won*, all of them having to do with desire, and all derived from the even more ancient *wen*. In English today, they echo in words like *wish, venal,* and *win*.

In Middle English, the word *venim* turned up. Today, it's *venom*. *Venison*, before it referred to the meat of the deer, was the word for the flesh of any animal taken in the hunt. The hunter in Old French was a *veneur*, and the hunting was *venerie*. In English, the word for the hunt became *venery*. The ideas of desire, hunting, wishing, struggling to gain and so on also underlie the word *win*. In Old English *winnan* meant to strive, struggle or fight. On the other hand *wynsum* referred to something pleasing, winning, or winsome.

Over several thousand years, a three-letter word for "love" was turned this way and that to give us words with as wide a range of meanings as *venomous* and *winsome, winning* and *venerating, venison* and a *wish* ... the goddess and planet *Venus*. From a single word unfolds a family of words, centuries of history and a procession of people who loved and seduced, hunted and struggled, bowed to gods and wished for things—our ancestors.

Our English linguistic ancestors originally spoke a form of German but they found Latin helpful, so a Latin word like *credo* ("I know") gave us *miscreant* (someone who's bad to know), *creed, credit, credentials* and *incredible* ... and *dies mal*, "bad days," the days that olden soothsayers calculated to be unlucky, gave us *dismal*; but *disaster* came from *dis-aster* or "ill-starred" and is a word that has amongst its relatives *astrophysics, astrology* and *asteroids*.

Noon—the ninth hour—was 3 p.m. under Roman reckoning. Early Christian monks keeping the canonical hours used to pray every day at that time: *nones*. When the service was brought back to midday, the name came with it and noon was no longer 3 o'clock.

To enter a language is to enter a maze-like museum that touches the distant past and the accumulated experiences of past generations. A great number of English words have come from other languages, and we're importing more. It adds poignancy to a barbecue to know that the word *barbecue* is a rare, surviving relict of the ill-fated Arawak people, indigenous to the West Indies. The Spaniards assimilated the word before they extirpated the culture, and the English borrowed Spain's *barbecue*.

In New Zealand, I watched this borrowing happen as words were drawn into everyday New Zealand English usage from Maori, and as place names commemorating minor English bureaucrats, administrators or Imperial wars and their heroes were dropped in favor of their old, pre-colonial Maori names: names that evoke stories and identities far richer in meaning and association.

EVEN in Britain, home of "the Queen's English," there are languages other than English that have words that could yet be picked up. While living in Scotland, I discovered Scots: a Germanic language that's closer than modern English to Old English. It has a wealth of wonderful, energetic words for social experiences that modern English finds hard to capture. Your *howff*, for example, is your favorite pub and to be *canty* is to be gregariously happy, ready to laugh or sing. Heartier yet, or a few pints later, you'll be *rantin'*. *Clarty* is dirty and *mingin'* is stinky. *Driech* is a word that captures the chill, misty-moist weather that Scotland's known for. But to *fash* yourself about it would be to work yourself up into a bother. And *blether* (related to *blithering* in English, meaning silly or pointless chatter) is a word I'd have often thought useful beyond Scotland's borders. Conversation with more intent and passion, but "without prejudice" (in the social as well as the legal sense), is *craic*—a time-honored tradition of banter in Glasgow pubs.

SOME words, of course, come about from people mimicking the sounds of the real thing: *cackle*, *bang*, *slap*, *drum*, *thud*, *snort* ... and some words arose by accident. An *orange* was once a Spanish *naranja*. In Middle English, an *apron* was a *napron* and an *adder* was a *nadder*. A *pea* was a *pease* but that sounded like more than one so the *-se* was dropped. Somebody got confused.

A ramble through an English pocket dictionary will take you to word sources around the world and back to prehistoric times. It will summon up the names of scarcely remembered gods and rulers, and evoke the farm practices, cottage-crafts and village lives of ancient peasants. Language binds us to our past and steers us into the future.

LANGUAGE is a lot more fun than we often care to remember.

It excites our imaginations because it triggers associations that rekindle memories and the emotions. It empowers us to hover between the particular and the general—and "meaning" becomes a unique personal experience.

We are, at our innermost depths, always alone. But a language others share puts us into constant companionship. Language and culture are indivisible. Both hold us in balance with a wider social context in which we'd otherwise be personally meaningless. A language gives the culture of which it is a part its main medium of expression and banner of identity. This is what is so cruel about the modernizing world's impact on languages and imperialism's deliberate assaults on indigenous languages. (It's been estimated that in the last 500 years, half of the old world's old languages have been driven to extinction.)

As a part of our life experience, the languages we speak and the experiences they open to us become a considerable part of who we are. Our experience through language and within language—spoken and written—becomes a vital force in all that shapes and sustains our "self".

And all of this, like the stories we make our own, brings us back to vexed questions about "truth."

>*Do we speak words?*
>*Or do words speak us?*

"A NEW WORD," TAMWORTH, ONTARIO

7
Wildernesses

"WILDERNESS," TAMWORTH, ONTARIO

WILDERNESS has to be thought to exist wherever you find it impossible to get by on your own terms, and where there's enough room in which to feel lost.

For many, true wilderness is imagined as a wild, untouched, romantically remote natural landscape. But ideas of "pristine" or "untouched by human hands" don't work. Even the deep ocean trenches, the furthest recesses of faraway caves, and the atmosphere's highest altitudes carry the shadows and scars of human activity. Scientists at the Institute of Marine Sciences in Barcelona found human food scraps and plastic microparticles in the guts of fish living more than 2,000 metres under the sea in the Valencia Trench. Of the 300 million tonnes of plastics produced annually, about a third is thrown away soon after it's used. It breaks down into microparticles. Some are locked away in sea ice, some collect in oceanic gyres, some sink and are eaten by marine life. There's enough of it around to start compromising the safety of seafoods.

> *The British Geological Survey tells us that some 57,000 million tonnes of earth and rock are shifted by human activity each year.*

> *This compares with the 22,000 million tonnes of sediment shifted by the world's seas and rivers. We move rock and soil in the course of mining, building, and industrial development, and inadvertently when farming and construction projects expose soil to erosion.*[46]

WILDERNESS is more truly a personally-defined experience. Inner-city New York—one of the world's most urbanized places—was a wilderness to Tepilit Ole Saitoti, the subject of a *National Geographic* documentary who'd grown up a Maasai warrior in Tanzania. Never before had he seen so many people. They thronged past him on the busy streets, seemingly oblivious to each other and their surroundings. "New Yorkers seldom talk to one another," he pointedly remarked. "They have everything, so nothing fascinates them."[47]

Ideally, "wilderness" is a more-than-human place that grants us solitude. Mine's the ocean and its restless motion. It's an inner precipice from which I feel compelled to leap every now and again to shake off the bonds of distraction. It launders my self-awareness and lets me meet life headlong again. It shatters whatever might have begun to confine me.

> *Thundering, tumbling, reaching:*
> *the surging, swelling, on-rushing*
> *arc of ocean's edge ...*
> *Birdsong stretches the air to fit the day;*
> *a warming web sheds diamonds of dew*
> *on the upturned wrist of dawn ...*
> *Bounding squirrel, clambering beetle ...*
> *A staring toad ... eyes, fleeting, met*
> *wild-wind dancing and blown rain....*
> *Hue's rising, blushing, extending*
> *uncurling, arraying, disclosing—*
> *as another blossom's chalice fills ...*
> *Firelight chasing, shadows dancing*
> *embers lingering, sparks leaping*
> *anticipations ... and aftertastes ...*
> *Infinity turning, night sky yawning ...*
> *far-off stars aching to be touched ...*
> *clouds like gauchos riding moonbeams ...*
> *How uselessly we'd name it,*
> *frame it, tame it, lame it, maim it ...*
> *How gainfully we breathe it in ...*
> *How well we do, to expel it:*
> *Ephemerally—as joy.*

OUR ancestor cultures of the West have mostly viewed "wilderness" with suspicion, as a threat. It's feared as chaotic and dangerous, as a wasteland, or seen as a monster to be caged, fled from or subdued: an obstacle to virtue. It exists as places of enchantment and transformation, where you can get lost and face mortal or spiritual perils. Wildernesses can land you in a lot of trouble.

Our folklore and popular culture teem with wilderness frights. Fauns and satyrs, centaurs and trolls have long rivalled each other in the game of driving mortals mad. Sanity has never really been defined, but insanity has and with fearsome consequences.[48]

The female *Baobhan Sith* of olden Scotland—just one of a host of night-stalking Celtic fiends—sucked the blood from wilderness trespassers. Remember Beowulf's fight against the terrifying Grendel? Grendel's wild, dark forest was populated by "wideor": wild beasts. It was at the edge of "wild-beast-scape" that Gilgamesh anciently fought the terrible Humbaba. Having killed him, Gilgamesh made city gates from the forest's cedars: order from perceived chaos.

More recently, in J.R.R. Tolkien's books, forests become vivid, unfixed, fantastical nightmares inspired by *Beowulf* and the author's experiences of trench warfare during the First World War. The theme is perpetuated, amplified and extended by filmmakers and by science fiction and horror writers.

So, for example, first-time Australian director Jennifer Kent got a rave response at the 2014 Sundance Festival for her horror hit *The Babadook*. In the movie, domesticity is turned to terror by a small boy's obsession with a character in a frightening pop-up book. But it's the boy's increasingly disturbed widowed mother who really powers up the shock levels. Deliberately or not, *The Babadook* impact owes everything to its exciting audience's intimate phobias about mental illness. The demons born of insanity appealed, mental illness of one sort or another afflicting an estimated 1-in-5 or more North Americans during their lifetime.

What we don't understand, what we can't control, we're likely to fear. Walls help to keep wilderness out. But, as the distressed princesses of folklore and fairy tale have so often found, even castle towers fail to keep determined witches, dragons and deceivers at bay.

It takes a handsome prince to save the day ... and rescue the innocent beauty with his death-dealing sword. Whether it's on low-budget horror movie sets or lavishly ornamented in Hollywood with special effects, the theme is repeated over and over, as pretty princesses and handsome knights plod the same old path to consummation.

The wilderness? It was to the wilderness that the witch banished the lovelorn Rapunzel. It was in the wilderness that the woodcutter's children, Hansel and Gretel, found the alluring home of a cannibal witch. It was in the wilderness that Snow White was abandoned, only to be cared for by dwarves, male dwarves. In an Italian variant of the story, she's "Bella Venezia," saved by robbers rather than dwarves. In such stories, forests teem with carnivorous trees, evil ravens, wolves, bears, sorcerers and witches, bandits, trolls, bad fairies, giants, gnomes, ogres, and other terrifying entities. At the story's end, they are either redeemed or, more often, lie dead at some valiant prince's feet, and everyone lives happily "ever after." If there's a woman around, she usually gets subdued too. The hero—because our culture has required that exemplars of order be generally male—is the one who saves pitiable princesses and children from chaotic forces and subjects them to his "happy ever after."

The ethos of asserting virtue by "defeating" an opponent saturates media coverage of political and sports events alike. So, after making the first ascent of Mt. Everest with his Sherpa, Sardar Tenzing Norgay, Sir Edmund Hilary announced their return to base camp with the words: "We knocked the bastard off." It's a way of seeing relationships that reduces the status of whatever's subdued, "defeated" or "knocked off," often with an implied allegation of moral or social inferiority.

The attitude underlies racism, supremacism and lingers even in some forms of "wilderness" and nature park management. It's implicit in desires, for example, to set a "park" apart as a separate region, then begin "improving" it with power outlets, vehicle access, car parks, and fire-breaks, Wi-Fi access, kitchen and ablution blocks, roped-off swimming areas and drive-in campsites.

But wilderness can't be that submissive, easeful, polite, safe or ordered and still be "wild." Wilderness is not about sightseeing. It does not provide relaxation. It is place of balance between terror, desire, tedium, loneliness, love, danger, mystery and assurance. Wilderness is a place of inner challenge and rediscovery. And, in all of its forms, it has a beauty that, once discovered, can be overwhelming and healing, even potentially lethal.

When a balance is found, it comes with a rush of exhilaration and restoration. The exhilaration may be the thrill of the "victor," at which point beauty recedes … or it may be a richer and deepened, transforming appreciation of life. This is a reasonably "true" experience of being "born again." Either way, though, there's never closure or completion. *Being*, one finds, is necessarily about *becoming*.

> *To have been introduced to caving at the age of 18 was an extraordinary gift. Many of the cave passages that run like arteries through New Zealand's limestone beds had yet to be discovered or explored so it was possible to venture into places no-one had ever been before, to be the first person to squeeze through narrow passages, climb into previously unseen chambers, wade or swim in mysterious riverbeds and pools, and stand under waterfalls that led we knew not where. We explored in small groups for safety's sake and the experiences of exquisite beauty in these hidden places were made more real by companionship: we affirmed each other's awe. Beauty was an inescapable part of every day spent underground: it revealed itself in the limited circles of light thrown by the sputtering carbide lamps on our helmets. And always, beyond the edge of darkness, there was more to be experienced. Sometimes we'd feel an urgency to push ahead; sometimes we'd long to linger.*

To a non-caver, it was all mystery. I, certainly, could never express, explain or describe the sights I'd seen, or their impacts on me, except to people who'd also been there. Beauty, I came to realize, is always like that: never sought, it may never be experienced; experienced, it becomes indescribable. But it changes those it seizes. It's everywhere and it fills me with gratitude.

OUR culture has long favoured victors; submission's been shameful.

So our tortured heroes of "wilderness" exploration have typically been unbending cavaliers of "civilization." They lugged around crates of food and drink, portmanteaux of clothing for every occasion, libraries, furniture, dinnerware, tents, carpets, weapons and ammunition. Sometimes, they portaged things like pianos and steel boats. They did not simply "travel"; they mounted and equipped *expeditions*. And they blazoned belittlement on savagery wherever they discerned it.

These were *Boy's Own* heroes like Henry Stanley (aka John Rowlands) and David Livingstone who inched their way around Africa with long baggage trains, brandishing axes, guns and machetes. They led columns of native "bearers" and threatened to shoot them if they baulked.

In March 1871, Henry Stanley set out to find the "lost" David Livingstone with 200 experienced porters. When they began to desert him, Stanley, not the most gracious of employers, began flogging those who stayed. Livingstone meanwhile found it politic to co-operate with slavers in his quest for the source of the Nile.

One of the less publicized members of the trans-American Lewis and Clark expedition was a young Lemhi-Shoshone mother, Sacagawea. She carried her baby boy, Jean-Baptiste, with her on her back. More than the actions of Lewis or Clark or their 31 accompanying soldiers, volunteers and interpreters, it was Sacagawea's knowledge, language, contacts and assurances of peaceful intent that secured the expedition's success. She died, unremarked outside of her own community, not long afterwards, in 1812.

We can think back to treasure seekers like Ferdinand Magellan, killed fighting in a local war in the Philippine Islands in 1521, or Hernan Cortez who, in the same century, devastated Aztec culture. Or Francisco Pizarro and Hernando de Soto who trashed the Incas. There was Alvar Nunez Cabeza de Vaca violently seeking gold in Florida, and Christopher Columbus, looking for Asia in the Caribbean.

Then there were Arctic adventurers, like Henry Hudson and John Franklin, who'd hoped to open a trade-advantaging Northwest Passage.

In what's politically been billed as a "mystery," Franklin and his ships vanished. But an Orcadian doctor working for the Hudson Bay Company, John Rae (*Aglookaa*: "long strider" in Inuktituk) was at the time exploring the northern Arctic coastline on foot. In fact, he effectively discovered the "Northwest Passage" long before climate change made it look a whole lot more navigable. John Rae's approach was based on respect towards the Inuit he met and came to know. He valued their skills, knowledge, culture and wisdom. Inuit became his friends. His achievements included learning the fate of Franklin's expedition and assembling a small collection of relics as evidence. Inuit hunters told him about finding about 30 European corpses and signs of cannibalism.

Reporting this, though, led to John Rae immediately being vilified by Lady Franklin and her supporters. Charles Dickens wrote a scathing denial of John Rae's report that included a vicious attack on Rae's "savage Esquimaux" sources. So, while English history celebrated Franklin as a martyr to exploration, John Rae died in obscurity.[49] The information and evidence he'd handed over was suppressed, and the "mystery" that he and his Inuit friends had resolved remained, officially, a mystery. It offended the sensibilities of the English establishment. But it also remained a mystery because Rae's narrative was sourced in a frightening, unpalatable and "godless" wilderness. Civilization's blindfold offered the more comfortable refuge of ignorance.

Other imperialist flag raisers—like James Cook, killed by Hawaiians—also won honour at home and became household names. Leading figures of the more recent "heroic age of Antarctic exploration" include Ernest Shackelton, Robert Falcon Scott and Roald Amundsen (who was greatly helped by John Rae's work).

Ludwig Leichart, Ernest Giles and Alfred Gibson perished in Australia, traversing country that had sustained Aboriginal peoples, generation upon generation, for 60,000 years. George Mallory and Andrew ("Sandy") Irvine died on the slopes of Everest in 1921, and Percy Fawcett vanished in Brazil in 1925.

But death in the cause has not necessarily been unwelcome. Missionary martyrs, from the days of Roman persecutions to the present, have found affirmations of faith in their fate, in much the same way that nations celebrate and commemorate the "sacrifice" of their military dead.

> *In my teens, I was taught to "read" the New Zealand bush. The undergrowth can make it impossible to see very far and, above it, tall trees reach into other worlds. Underfoot, in deep shade, layers of leaves turn slowly to soil. It's possible to hike through it and see very little. But, lie in silence on the fallen leaves, close your eyes and listen and, after a minute or two of stillness, the sounds begin telling their stories. The thick press of plants becomes transparent. Agile little birds sieve rays of sunlight for flying insects, tweetering as they dart this way and that; others scour tree bark and foliage for prey. Some sip nectar from flowers in the canopy and sing out for mates or to stake territorial claims. The nectar-loving "tui" has region-specific calls—in time you can learn to locate yourself from their songs. Fruit eaters, typically plump wood pigeons, their flight more audible than their soft cooing, announce a season of ripeness. With an ear pressed to the leaf-mould, I've heard centipedes and large carabid beetles scritch their way toward prey. At night, small hunting owls, kiwis, wetas (handsome insects resembling*

crickets) and destructively omnipresent opossums get active. I learned a lot about listening from birds. The whole fabric of bush life is somehow held together acoustically. And, as the meanings of the sounds emerge, wilderness becomes intimate loveliness.

THEN there are travellers, curious enthusiasts drawn to wonder by the richness of cultures other than their own: people like Sir Richard Burton, the admirably flawed "Ugly Englishman" who visited Mecca and translated the *One Thousand and One Nights* from Arabic.

Strabo of Amasia (part of modern Turkey) travelled and wrote in the time of Caesars Augustus and Tiberius. He produced an encyclopaedic 17-book *Geographica*: a mass of observations, research and investigations to do with the Roman world of his day. He called this work his "colossal creation": his *Kolossourgia*.[50]

In the second century, Pausanias described his observations of Greece in a more personable style.[51] His 10-volume *Hellados Periegesis* includes first-hand experiences and local myths, religious ideas and oral history, plants, wildlife and wonders in ways that make it clear he was in conversation with people, listening to them, gathering human and natural details and bringing that vividness to the ancient landscape he was documenting.

There was the seventh century Chinese monk Xuanzang who patiently trekked 10,000 miles along the northern route of the Silk Road, studying and collecting Buddhist texts to enlighten, not only himself, but also his countrymen. With the tall backpack he carried to protect the precious scrolls he gathered, he returned to China after 16 years on the road to write a unique account of Central and South Asia.

In the more recent past, we've seen traveller-writers like Wilfred Thesiger, Isabella Lucy Bird, Freya Stark, Peter Matthiesen, László Almásy, Nicolas Bouvier, Jacques Cousteau, Dervla Murphy, Eric Newby, William Dalrymple, Bruce Chatwin, Kira Salak, Benedict Allen, and many others: people who've travelled to learn and listen, willing to be personally engaged, challenged and changed.

They represent an antithesis to the likes of the Irish whisky magnate James Sligo Jameson, a member of Stanley's mission to find David Livingstone. He sated his vicarious fascination with cannibalism by buying a 10-year-old slave girl for six handkerchiefs, then handing her over to cannibals on the condition that he be allowed to watch and sketch their culinary prep. The girl was duly tied, bled out, butchered, cooked and eaten while Jameson produced half a dozen watercolor illustrations of the proceedings.

Few have turned popular misinformation to greater profit than Walt Disney, the billionaire anthropomorphist, one of whose characteristically despicable acts was to have a special centrifuge built to fling lemmings over a cliff so his cameras could record a popular but false folk myth. He used every cinematic device he could lay his hands on to misrepresent "wild" as "fluffy" in a profits-driven onslaught to tell people what they wanted to hear. But, although he did so much to cultivate incomprehension, I find Walt Disney most objectionable for his stunting of so many people's capacity for wonder and awe. He deflated these two significant emotions to a safe little suburban headspace called "cute," as opposed to "yucky." Cartoon puppies, kittens, bunnies, seal pups, flying elephants, deer, chipmunks and squirrels are "cute"; plankton, insects and snakes are "yucky." This is at least partly why so few people are worried about the dramatically declining global levels of phytoplankton: major fixers of carbon and producers of oxygen, and the foundation of oceanic food chains. Plankton aren't cute. Nor are pollinators or pest-controlling bats or snakes ... creatures that are also experiencing declines. Unlike "beauty," which challenges, transfixes and transforms whoever seriously approaches it, "cute" is non-threatening, uninformative, fleeting and disposable. "Cute" is a perfect word of patronization. It leaves ignorance utterly unruffled. "Beauty" is its towering opposite: irreconcilable with anything that would oppress or debase it ... a bastion of truth. The wild is our ancestral home, the shaper of our highest and our basest selves. It's our birthright: complicated and exciting, and real. We'd lock it up if we could. But we can't, not wholly, despite the efforts of a multibillion-dollar entertainment industry, the construction of monstrous, noisy, smelly cities, the ability to move at speeds that turn reality into a passing blur ... constant chatter and incessant stimulation. So, more and more, we're inclined to fear what we must embrace. Denial may feel good but the walls of the comfort zone are tissue-thin and what we fail to see, or choose not to see, will not reverse or change course. It just keeps coming and when the tissue disintegrates, "Yikes," as Mickey Mouse might exclaim, are we ever surprised. Nature simply IS. It knows no "cute" or "icky." It is life. It is implacable, and it is invincible. Nature can wipe us off the face of the planet the moment we cross the line without a thought about collateral damage. The "wild" does not depend on us. It will smother our children before it lets us destroy the planet. Do you really think nature mourns the dodo? No more will it lament our passing, or the collapse of our proudest achievements, if that's what we choose to bring on ourselves.

ODDLY, you might think, it's in the Judaeo-Christian tradition that wilderness turns up, at least partly, as a blessing.

Azazel, the archetypal scapegoat, was burdened with others' evil, cursed and banished to lurk in the waterless wilderness, yes.

But the wilderness has also been held dear as a place of transcendent experience set apart from society's failings and distractions: a place to rediscover "god." Jesus is said to have spent "forty days and forty nights" fasting in the desert in preparation for his ministry. For many early Christian hermits, ascetics and monks it was a place of holy austerity. Their communities sprang up in the North African desert, so many choosing this harsh but spiritually irresistible path to enlightenment that Saint Athanasius, in the fourth century, described Egypt's Nitrian desert as "a city."

In the thirteenth century, Saint Francis (Giovanni di Pietro di Bernardone), recognising the souls of wild animals, saw them as his equals before god. In the forests around Assisi, he preached to them as he did to his human companions. He taught that it was a human duty to protect and enjoy nature.

> *The light that flickers through the leaves,*
> *The light that skips off breaking waves*
> *The light that sprawls on mountain snows*
> *The light that sparkles from the lake*
> *The light that fades full-colored at the end of day ...*
> *This light is not the light we see in our cities*
>
> *It is not the light that stares along highways at night*
> *It is not the light that fails to fade the furniture*
> *It is not the light that chops up the night*
> *It is not the light we curl up with in bed*
> *It is not the light that's doused with a switch*
> *This light is not the light.*
>
> *It is the light that calls the world to life*
> *It is the light that startles us in nakedness*
> *It is the light that raises up the trees.*
> *It is the light that's always been*
> *It's the light that makes us humble*
> *It's the light that may yet make us good*

DEATH's a wilderness we all face. After death, who knows? Near-death experiences are rare but seem to be overwhelmingly tranquill, no matter what pain's been felt up to that point. Perhaps they're nothing more than side effects of our physiological processes shutting down. Or they may point to something altogether less likely.

The first medical account of a near death experience was published in 1776 by a French military doctor, Pierre-Jean du Monchaux. One of his patients who'd slipped into prolonged unconsciousness finally awoke and described seeing "such a pure and extreme light that he thought he was in the Kingdom of the Blessed." Never, he said, had he experienced a nicer moment.

Neurologist Steven Laureys heads the Coma Science Group at the Sart Tilman Liège University Hospital, Belgium. It's a job in which he hears about more near-death experiences than most people, and from a wider variety of near-fatal crises, ranging from cardiac arrest to drowning and head injuries. Like others who've recorded them, he's found them accompanied by surprisingly consistent feelings of reassuring peacefulness. Out-of-body experiences are often described, and an altered sense of time.[52]

Other accounts have been laden with cultural and religious interpretations—it's been suggested that they've informed shamanistic traditions—and, at an underlying level, overwhelmingly positive, even euphoric, feelings are typical.[53]

So let's not be too afraid of death....

> *The dark that softens the starkness of day*
> *The dark that stalls our minds in sleep*
> *The dark that calls the fireflies out*
> *The dark that rolls out space and stars*
> *The dark that opens paths to mystery ...*
> *This dark is not the darkness we see in our cities*
>
> *It is not the dark that heightens our fears*
> *It is not the dark that masks cold malice*
> *It is not the dark that saddens cell or tomb*
> *It is not the dark that has us suffer alone*
> *It is not the dark that's slain with a switch*
> *This dark is not the dark.*
>
> *It is the dark that calls the world to hush*
> *It is the dark that makes our shame less sharp*
> *It is the dark that becomes a theatre of dreams*
> *It is the dark that's always been*
> *It's the dark that makes us still enough to see*
> *It's the dark that may yet make us whole.*

NOR, more importantly for the moment, need we fear life. Life too is first and foremost a wilderness. And "wilderness" is what sex should be: impossible on one's own terms, a source of awe and wonder.

That it doesn't always play out that way has a lot to do with the sorts of cultural, psychosocial and emotional cracks that have opened over the centuries, allowing us to fetishize sex as idylls in our own image or imagination.

The sexual impulse has, at its source, a chemically regulated goading to get on with enough biological exertion to perpetuate the species. The complicated feelings of pleasure, torment and longing that accompany it can help us humans bond with each other, ideally for as long as our progeny need us around. But, let loose among our overly complicated psychologies, sex has become one of our most recklessly trampled wildernesses.

Human sexuality has been expressed in countless ways and attained enormous existential significance by inspiring artists and dreamers. It has shaped rituals, manners, aesthetics, legislation, social attitudes and cultural norms. Some of that, it must be admitted, has been has been disastrous and, rather like the mindset of the imperialist adventurer, some of it has been viciously self-absorbed, ignorant, evil and extreme.

It's not just the overly complicated psychology we bring to it that makes it problematic. It's our spirituality, or want of it, our culture, our ambivalence towards experiences of wilderness, and our feelings of entitlement. Our functionally oriented education system doesn't help: it can take the edge off our openness to imaginative engagement and leave us dulled by regimentation.

Viktor Frankl wrote: "True encounter is based on self-transcendence rather than mere self-expression."[54] It's also is the key to self-knowledge which, though it may not always be flattering, is always liberating.

When self-entitlement and self-ignorance are expressed by way of sexuality, as a form of consumption, the result's an often destructive form of violence. It's the violence of the fashion advertiser, the entertainment industry, the pimp and the pornographer; it's the violence of the bigot, the bully and the rapist. Its victims have usually but not always been women, the weak, the poor and those with minority sexual orientations.

> As a child, I loved poring over the family atlas. I'd find and then try to find out about a place I'd never imagined before ... like, say the little baseball-crazy community of Carolina, Puerto Rico, where the poet Julia de Burgos was born. Or 6,000-year-old Plovdiv in Bulgaria, from which I later went on to discover Gela—one of the mythological birthplaces of Orpheus, high in the Rhodope Mountains. I've since been there, to meet a master Bulgarian bagpipe (kaba gaida) player, "Bai" Dafo Trendafilov. I spoke no Bulgarian; he and his family spoke no English but I was warmly welcomed me and fed, and he played his magical music to me as the sun set behind the mountains. His playing is immortalized on a solid gold recording that was launched into space in 1977 with the Voyager 1 spacecraft. But, all around the world, there are families and individuals with gifts, joys and worries, hopes and satisfactions, and open hearts who get up every morning and go about their day in ways we can't begin to visualize until we go there.

RODERICK Frazier Nash was the first person to raft down California's beautiful

Tuolumne River. Wilderness, he has argued ever since, teaches us the value of humility.

"My purpose is to persuade you that wilderness is a moral resource," he wrote in a *New Scientist* article in 2002: "Civilisation severed the web of life as humans distanced themselves from the rest of nature. Behind fenced pastures, village walls and, later, gated condominiums, it was hard to imagine other living things as relatives, or nature as sacred.

"The remaining hunters and gatherers became 'savages.' The community concepts, and attendant ethical respect, that had worked to curb human self-interest in dealings with nature declined in direct proportion to the 'rise' of civilisation. Nature lost its significance as something to which people belonged and became something they possessed: an adversary, a target, and an object for exploitation.

"The resulting war against the wilderness was astonishingly successful. Today we have fragments of a once-wild world. The ark is sinking and on our watch. In the biblical past people went to the wilderness to receive the commandments with which to restructure society. We need to do so again."[55]

Nash's 1989 book, *The Rights of Nature: A History of Environmental Ethics*,[56] has become an inspiration for new work towards environmental ethics. It's about time: in just 40 years, human activities erased over half of our world's wildlife. In the past 500 years, we have unleashed extinction on at least 300 known species.

The distinguished "father of sociobiology" and double Pulitzer Prize winner Edward O. Wilson urges us to secure our survival and earth's biodiversity by turning half of the world's surface over to undisturbed nature, and to restrict ourselves to just the other half.[57] This would curb mass extinctions and let natural selection continue at the levels both of individual species and of groups. It's probably a political impossibility—already there's very little land or ocean that isn't deeply compromised by human activity—but he is right to assert that the biosphere does not belong to us.

> *It's at sea level that we get as close to the horizon as it's possible: about three miles. And, when we sail three miles towards it in one direction, we are no closer; our wake trails away to the gathering horizon behind us. We are enclosed. It's the stars that tell us that we have moved over the face of our planet. And, unaided by technology, we see stars only at night. And unlit night is delicious mystery.*

THE more I experience wilderness, the closer I'm nudged towards thinking that, in truth, everywhere is potential wilderness. It's defined by our anxieties. Roderick Nash put it this way: "Rightly seen, wilderness is the best demonstration that we are not the only, or even the primary, members of the biotic team (life forms). It is a living reminder of the gross limitations of our definitions of 'society' and 'morality'. Our real society is coterminous with life on this planet, a fact that our ethical sensibilities have as yet failed to recognize."

We've tried to hold wilderness in check. But don't attempts to impose our terms and conditions on the world around us always come unstuck in the end?

Maybe that's why my *Thesaurus* has so few apt antonyms for wilderness but so many synonyms. Wilderness—embraced and accepted it as it is, rather than as we might like it to be—has the wonderful power to evaporate a lot of the vanities and illusions that make life a misery. And, given a freer rein, wilderness makes spiritual impressions as well as moral ones. The difficulty, I find, is that it's getting harder to access wilderness, despite its being all around me: social fragmentation hides it, it's denied by the rising volume of noise and irrelevancies, and by the disconnectedness that's all around. Dropping thought and feeling into the high-speed blender that life's become hides the seamlessness. We're left in social environments that flicker as though under disco lights, and hide meaning's whispers behind the pounding beats of so many unbearable urban lifescapes.

The difference between *wilderness* and *mystery*? Wilderness is the vehicle, and a motive; mystery is the experience that makes it matter. That is my motive for seeking the ocean. It's what I miss most when I am away from it: the embrace of a straight-edged encircling horizon that draws introspection out to an elemental fullness, and collapses it into the simple awareness of unconditional existence.

> TANGAROA (The Sea God)
> I was eight years old when
> Tangaroa ate my heart
> and in that moment gave me
> my home: the horizon.
>
> My home surrounds me:
> seen, unseen, a hairline
> between the sea and sky
> without a place to rest
>
> So to everything's edge
> I have ferried my soul
> and at everything's edge
> I have feasted on delight.

8
Religion

"ZDENYK'S WELCOME TO STRAKONICE," REPUBBLICA CECA (CZECH REPUBLIC)

SCARED? In a strange country, bounded by a language I don't understand and trying to catch onto ways that are at odds with those I'm used to, I've found it helpful to look at the poor: the beggars, the street peddlers. Their society's heart is etched in their faces and posture. And it's good to listen to local musicians, if they can be found, and to go to a religious gathering: a church, a duomo, a mosque, a synagogue, a chapel, a basilica, a temple, a cathedral.

There, as unobtrusively as I can, I follow along with whatever everyone else is doing: I've kissed icons, taken eucharists, inhaled smudging smoke and incense, eaten what's offered, shaken hands and shared hugs, knelt or sat in silence and touched my forehead to the floor; I've clapped, lit candles, danced, attended funerals, and sung hymns *sotto voce* in syllables suggested by the voices around me. I've been there for less than an hour; I've been there for five or six hours, and it's all felt like time well spent. It's stuff no one can tell you about and that you won't read in a guidebook.

An explicit bodily experience accompanies ritual. It doesn't explain anything but it can convey a lot about the quality of being behind a sense of place. It's a low-information, high-content narrative that adds insight to exploration. It draws me to people; my curiosity has always been welcomed, and taking part has given me a short cut, a snapshot, a dip into the essence of the local culture. Sometimes, it's led me on to people's homes and celebrations, and opened new friendships.

CULTURES don't draw conclusions the way individuals do. Rather, they steer our interactions. Religions are a little different: they engage us with life, and with each other. Few of the popular definitions stretch around all of the activities that anthropologists and religious adherents would want to include. Some religious activities happen privately in contemplative silence; some are boisterously public.

Despite what they say, religions aren't all about "belief." It would be a lot simpler if they were. Belief is something you could fit into a 20-second YouTube clip. But the religions I've seen something of have the characteristics of an ongoing debate, or a cacophony of debates. It's invariably hard to find two "believers" who agree about very much at all. Typically, the most committed of the "faithful" diverge to form schools, traditions, sects, denominations, orders, factions, branches and orthodoxies.

Most religions have long histories of intimate interaction with their societies, drawing people in with one breath and expelling them with the next; attraction and alienation, belief and rejection, attention and denial, faith and fanaticism, care and control, poverty and power, caution and abandon... in and out, in and out. But worship, music, ritual, metaphor—every variety of spiritual empathy—are formed in the same kettles of human need, emotion, anxiety, joy and spirituality. So, despite everything, after entering into some of those moments, a traveller's likely to feel closer, more open and easy there than among all of the inhibitions that govern the street.

Religion is aspiration by way of analogy. It's about hopes of integrating oneself with a grand plan that's only ever imperfectly understood because, although it's about everyday human interactions, it's scaled to perspectives beyond imaginings: it's a lifetime search for more than a life. Religions—when they're in good working order—help to free people from spiritual snares and turn simple ways of living into theatres of inspiration and adventure. Again, if their integrity's intact, they reveal hope, beauty and promise.

The so-called "great religions" carry massive payloads of lore, history and wisdom that speak in a variety of voices to people in an even greater array of personal circumstances. Wisdom's great value may be its resilience, proven over time, but it can't be casually flexed to meet market demands. Religions' historical momentum makes the fine-tuning of faith to the motley, changing cultures they're a part of an ever-wobblier preoccupation. The links between concentrated religious insight, spirituality and ritual have to be kept fresh. Generation by generation, they need to resonate with the accelerating flows of community life without uprooting their core insights from the deeper, less mutable character of all humanity.

That's a tall order. Pragmatic minds have tried to regularize spirituality within the confines of organized religion and for all time. In 325, Rome's first Christian emperor, Constantine I, called a summit in the Anatolian city of Nicea to regularize a statement of belief. This resulted in the Nicene Creed, which gave answer to the question put to Jesus by Pontius Pilate, prefect of Roman Judea: "what is truth?"[58] Statements of belief turn faith to dogma. They define and create a focus on error, heresy, dissent, apostasy, schismatism and nonconformity ... and Christianity was rife with controversies from the start. There's nothing like imposed consistency and sound sense to shatter a faith's unity. So, in 380, the Edict of Thessalonica made Christianity the one state religion of the Roman Empire. Just five years later, in 385, Pricillian, the ascetic bishop of Avila in Spain, and six of his followers were tortured and executed by other Christians for heresy. Then, just a few more years later, he and those who died with him were being eulogized as martyrs.

Organizing religion is as silly as storing water in a sieve. But, because they have clear form, because they are visible, it's sieves that have too often become the foundations and fabric of religious practice. And sieves can exclude what they don't already contain. Sooner or later, organized religions find the exclusion working against them.

Meanwhile, modernity's relativism is whittling society's old list of widely felt values and experiences back to fewer and fewer encompassing social forces. Religion is at the edge.

> *THERE was a place we liked to go to in Central Scotland: a deceptively accessible lookout that archaeologists identify as a 5,500-year-old burial and ceremonial mound: Cairnpapple. From its summit, you can see the full span of Scotland's narrow waist: the low-lying land between the Firth of Forth and the estuary of the Clyde. I imagined Roman engineers standing here to decide the course of the Antonine Wall they would build. To the south, there'd be polity and order; to the north, chaos. Before the Romans, local people looking down from Cairnpapple would have vividly seen the layout of their own fields in relation to those of their neighbours and their surroundings. There could have been no "surprise" approaches to their homes and the view must have enhanced their sense of "place" and particularity in a wider landscape. This high place instilled an awareness of power. So often has a Moses ascended such a high place and come down with new insight and rekindled authority. There actually IS a clearer view to be had from the mountaintop. And a clearer view is potent. It can be culturally momentous. Mount Sinai is associated with Moses to this day. Hawaiians reverenced the five volcanic peaks of their islands, which had the added charisma of periodic eruptions; the twin peaks of Nanda Devi in the Garhwal Himalayas are revered;*

China's cloud-topped Huangshan is "holy," and the Mount of Olives, where Jesus went to pray and meditate before his arrest, overlooks the biblically significant Kidron Valley. Machu Picchu was sacred to the Incas; the Black Hills, sacred to the Lakota Sioux, have become a tourist draw; Mount Athos in Greece is also known as "holy mountain," and Olympus was home to the ancient gods of Western civilisation. Mount Fujiyama holds tremendous significance for the people of Japan. And so it goes. The "clearer view" is seldom solely pragmatic. It can inspire insights, awe and reflection. As a youngster, I used to go climbing in New Zealand-Aotearoa, mostly on the slopes of the North Island's volcanic peaks. I found summits—even in cloud—always inspired a strange, freeing, often exhilarating feeling of "apartness": apart from time, apart from trivialities and immediate anxieties. Apart, alone and aware.

COULD religion have something to do with trying to share the focus and power of the mountaintop? Could its most vital role be to offer a place from which to take a fresh perspective on life, on oneself, apart from the snares of day-to-day distractions, practicalities and opportunities? A place of reflection? A place where we can sit among "gods" and hope to see ourselves as freely and clearly as they might?

CULTURES all have dark sides—sleeping demons—that can flare up when the culture is stressed. But a healthy culture is a fluent intermediary among people, and between its members and their wider world. It bends, it moves, it adapts. It assimilates, appropriates, integrates and affirms; it channels and harmonizes skills, insights, technologies, resources and aesthetics; it empowers communities and generates coherent arrays of motivations, roles, dependencies, norms, values, ethics and satisfactions; it quickens and shapes its members' relationships with their social and natural environments, and gives meaning to the actions of individuals. It allays fears, it celebrates life, and it provides everyone with a responsive context for the whole of life. Ideally, it can be trusted to take care of its members without having to be overly explicit. Its members don't need to know it all. It governs through sets of values that are self-evident to its members. They see them nourishing the good of the whole and managing the stresses that arise. Religions usually do quite well in healthy cultures.

But, when a culture comes apart, or is torn to pieces by another, the human costs are usually devastating. It can feel like the end of the world. And religions that misread the culture with which they're enmeshed with will fail too.

We live near the 235-kilometre course of the Salmon River, not far from where it rises on the Precambrian Shield. It cuts south through sheets of Ordovician limestone to pour anything from a trickle to 300 cubic metres of water a minute into Lake Ontario. Every day, the river has a different voice. I like to stand beside it, at about the same place, close my eyes and simply listen. The sounds resolve into something very like music, but freer. And it's never quite the same. The channel it has cut and the broken rock do not shift on a timescale of days, so it's the water, its dancing flow and the feelings I bring to it, that make the difference as it passes on its way to the lake. On the other hand, the water that flows from our taps here comes from a well. It is crystal-clean, cool and delicious. We live in what specialists call a "fractured rock" environment and our well is drilled 30 metres or so into it, down into a water-world far larger and more complicated than the singing river on the surface. Imagine utter darkness, caverns, canyons, cataracts and chambers, still reservoirs and rushing rivers: there are flows here, large, enduring and labyrinthine, that I can only imagine. Yet it is these flows, the flows I cannot see or hear, that physically sustain me, quench my thirst and support the community that's grown up here beside the beautiful river.

ANTHROPOLOGISTS have never documented a society that's devoid of religion. Religious susceptibility seems embedded in the "normal" human psyche. That said, religion's origins are vague. We can wonder about the spiritual world of the people who, 8,000 to 9,500 years ago, spent their lives in Çatalhöyük, a Neolithic community on Turkey's Konya Plain, or those who dwelt among the impressive buildings and statuary of Göbekli Tepe,[59] a Neolithic settlement in southeastern Anatolia 2,000 years older yet.

We can accept that scholars' conclusions about these people are reasonable. And we can surmise, along with many archaeologists, that what's known of burial practices 300,000 years ago could well be indicative of religious or proto-religious thought. But we can't pretend to grasp the essence of those thoughts or the spiritual experience of those ancient ancestors, or witness what they expressed within their communities.

MY view would be that language pretty much ensured the existence of religion. Language is a unique tool. Nothing else bonds people more closely, widely and usefully as a shared language. Nothing but language more strongly unites sensation, imagination and community.

The words we learn as infants, it's been shown, determine the way we divide experience into parts—like Lego pieces—and assert their "meanings." They become our conceptual building blocks. Words generate flows of understanding, yes. But they are flows of culturally-bounded understanding. People getting together, talking, thinking, hungry or feasting, dreaming, loving, watching and observing, experiencing life's mysteries, looking for companionship, co-operating, sharing fears and hopes and insights, remembering, singing, dancing, and weaving stories around it all ... all of it rests on words, words that shape and sustain worldviews, always circumscribed by a culture, a society. Shared values, ethics, wonder, art, risks, narratives, reasons, jokes and explanations—all are conveyed by language. And we are governed by it, if only to the extent of being made visible by it, and being able to negotiate it.

Searches for shared meaning prompt the telling of stories. Hero-figures and narratives coalesce around a name; values and ideals become explicit. Stories are drawn into each other as myths; myths intertwine to become the bodies of thought we identify as "truth." A culture comes to life as rising generations find that its truths parallel their own experience. The stupid stuff, for the most part, gets discarded. Symbols, metaphors, imagery and poetry give elasticity to ideas that might otherwise be too rigidly or narrowly understood.

The idea of a god or gods able to overcome the damage we do and punish us for doing it, or simply to toy with our lives, cannot have been the silliest way to face the mystery and vagaries of fate that engulf every experience we fail to understand.

At the core of it all, religions offer narratives that give meaning to personal and social existence, and fix reference points for accumulating wisdom. They give existence its conceptual substance.

"God" is a hypothesis that lets us talk about mystery. To talk about "god" or "the gods" is to examine the human condition and its meaning. "God" is, by definition, unknowable. Assertions about the nature of "god" diminish the point, purpose and meaning of what can become a part of the conversation. But "god" as a context for experience lets us feel empowered to reach beyond our egocentrism and see ourselves as we might be or become.

Religion should incline us to enter more deeply and fully into the phenomena of life and consciousness. Like science, it should help us to ask better questions. It should be a dynamic not a dogma. And it has been, and continues, in its finest times, to be exactly that. Sickened, stressed, it can get ugly.

WISDOM differs from knowledge in that, while knowledge accumulates information to find the core and essence of existence, wisdom whittles away irrelevancies towards the same end. Both have their goals, boundaries and limitations as well as their rewards. Methodologies differ.

In wisdom's case, the tales of one generation have passed on to the next, and the next, with the good sense of first-hand experience as its mediating force. It's not about obedience to an inviolate text; it's about path-finding, adaptation and transformation. The story telling, memorization, dream-sharing, ritual, questioning and discussion that go on in an oral culture articulate fresh insight.

Emphasizing understanding over detail, oral cultures and primal religions typically "form" rather than "instruct" people. A Polynesian navigator, for example, was not some guy who learned the techniques of navigation, but someone who became a navigator. It worked extremely well. Polynesians settled every inhabitable island in the eastern Pacific Ocean long before Europeans found their way into its expanses.

In some cultures, adepts become "shape shifters," relocating their spiritual and psychological vantage point to see more deeply into themselves and into nature. In our culture, we generally just "get a job." Only the fortunate find a "role." There are deep cognitive differences.

IT'S reasonable to think of a religion as having been informed by interactions with "mystery" over thousands upon thousands of years. But, because it's propagated collectively but experienced individually, you shouldn't expect to be met more than half way when you approach a religious tradition. Once wisdom reaches a certain depth and level of complexity, though, some kind of full-time oversight tends to be needed. So societies may install specialists: priests, rabbi and shamans. It's necessary to remember that these people may be leaders but they are not the ultimate arbiters of religion.

Finding faith takes time and patience. You do the hard stuff yourself. It's not like a club where a membership fee buys access to all of the privileges. A religion just opens a way, a path to fulfilment—and a bit of fun. Or it may not work for you at all.

ONLY after writing came along do we find the threads of a story to start to pick up. Religious thought had already developed beyond its sources by then and it's still hard to access. Indeed, it may be harder now than ever before.

We've been making hasty shifts into new, very different realms of experience and thought. And maybe that's enough to persuade some people to write religion off as unnecessary bunk in these "modern" times.

The mystery, though, is absolute and enduring. Moreover, our planet seems to need the sorts of transforming disciplines that religions have developed.

Summer hayshine afternoon ...
stagger-stiff from slinging bales
the boy is sent to get the cows,
rolling, gentle, heaving things,
sweeter scented than the hay ...
turning to close a gate, his bare foot
shocked
startles him with the feel
of fresh cow manure
and overcomes him with its goodness.

> *The wood of the gate is alive in his hands*
> *the grass swims like emerald fish*
> *the smells become a carnival*
> *that embraces the fat ambling clouds*
> *high, high on their blue pastures.*
> *Both feet now, toes working the dung*
> *the boy tastes transcendence*
> *for the first time in his life.*
> *But his father, laughing, says:*
> *"Shit, Robert. You're covered in shit."*

BECAUSE of religion's ducking and diving, twisting and turning, its varied practices and its complexity, rational academic inquiry has found it very difficult to define. In his book *The World until Yesterday* (2012), ethno-biologist Jared Diamond boldly cited 16 different definitions of religion, none of them especially helpful. This can suggest that religion is so compulsively erratic it can only be false.

Or it can be seen as academic failure to get the point. Or a bit of both.

A wrongheaded view is tempting. After all, the quirks of religious expression usually strike outsiders as bizarre and contradictory, even within a familiar culture, even within a single "religion." A Catholic High Mass, with its distanced ritual and fixed liturgy, is very different from a loud and emotional Pentecostal prayer meeting, or the often largely silent reflections of the Religious Society of Friends (Quakers), yet all three are Christian.

There are rifts between and among Shia, Sunni and "Sufi" (Tasawwuf) Muslims; Buddhism has many schools; and the world's primal "nativistic" religions offer even wider constellations of variety. The names and natures of god and gods are countless. Yet god is not an essential religious concept. It's all about meaning.

> *There's a centuries-old story—it originated in India but is now widespread and well known—about half-a-dozen blind men who each inspect then draw very different conclusions about the nature of an elephant. It's wisdom that's found in a more sophisticated form in the Medicine Wheel of North American native cultures: that we see the centre differently, depending on where we take our seat in the Circle. And we see opposed certainties at work every day in our communities, societies, nations and global politics. But something drives us in the modern West—and elsewhere—to insist that only ONE point of view can be "correct." In extreme times, we'll kill to make the point. We're not good at tolerating others' truths, despite the fact that only through diversity can human beings hope to survive on a planet that's too complicated, interconnected and vulnerable to satisfy us all if we all want the same*

thing in abundance, at the same time, or for all time. Hope, it seems to me, always lies with the dissidents and the diversities in our midst, no matter how well today's orthodoxy seems to meet the demands of the moment.

MOST perplexing to a modern mind, indoctrinated in rational explanation and quantifiable realities, is the language of religion: it seems foolish and naive. Its reaching after subjective depths of meaning, its dialogues of abstraction; its insistence on "spirit" and "transcendence" lead nowhere certain. It all looks like a waste of time. And it all seems archaic because, well ... it usually is. Religions don't explain themselves very well.

The Enlightenment shunted European languages headlong into particularism, literalism, reductionism and logical empiricism: it gained mechanistic power, but at the cost of its poetic potency. The faeries abandoned the olden landscape, and that segment of the Christian religion that fell under reason's sway became literalistic.

In attempting to defend and justify its sources, rather than furthering its address to the spirit, it joined the rush to celebrate the human mind. Literalism called either for revisionism or unreason. Both tried to force wisdom into logicality. Harder to access and less available, it was dismissed as naivety.

Christianity became increasingly divided and inept. Literalistic fundamentalism fed judgmentalism and bigotry, even violence. Focused on others' "evils," this sort of mis-religion turned many people away from the enduring challenges of mystery, self-knowledge, forgiveness and loving practice, even their own spirituality.

Religions affirm experience over observation: it's what you become, not what you think—so it's at the level of first principles that empiricist academic rigor and religion part ways. Religion's an art more than a discipline, even in its "disciplines." "God," "gods" and spiritual "goodness" are less like nouns (things) than verbs (activities): they identify ongoing engagement; they acknowledge our needs to become fully human. The word best suited for this necessary epicentre of religion is "faith." And, again, it's an action, not a thing: faith of necessity is a solitary journey.

Organized religion survives as companionship on bad faith days, and as a source of traditional wisdom, but none of it matters if its adherents are spiritually static, numbed or oblivious.

> *As children, we played year-round on the beach and in the sea. It was where we adventured, learned and slowly matured. Everything we could imagine was there: excitement, life, sun and wind and, if we felt hungry, we helped ourselves to shellfish, digging them from the sand or knocking them from the rocks and eating them raw. I feasted on oysters that are now beyond my means to*

buy. I began diving with a mask and snorkel when I was eight or nine, sailing and surfing when I was around 12. It was all just a part of lives attached to the sea. The sea for me, back then in my youth, was more than a playground; it was a schoolroom. A shark under water is one of the most breathtakingly beautiful creatures alive. To be peered at and appraised by the small, dark, cow-like eye of an orca just feet away was to be compelled by that stare to know that there's a consciousness there, far more attuned to the sea than I could ever be. It changed my sense of selfhood. I found I could know and be known by families of reef fish. From fish, I learned about risk and what a "food chain" is: fish live in a predator-prey world, a perilous relationship that's made endurable by satiation (getting full) and circumstance. Prey fish and penguins have no fear of a shark that's recently fed. A hunting shark emanates different energies that are unmistakable. This points to a tragic human failing: we're not arrested by satiation the way a shark is; crueler and more voracious, we'll munch on and on, and gather up more and more; we approach consumption competitively and pointlessly, like addicts; we are not rational. I've come to a view that beauty is god's language of love, no matter what "god" is, and that requiring oneself to seek out and enter into experiences of beauty is the key to all of the "Edens" that surround us. They enter us when we let them in—we don't enter them. The key that opens us to them is curiosity. I've become aware of a vast, unknowable but immediately present reality that envelops all of the dimensions that open to casual attention. It's as if what we inhabit in the busy "everyday" is just the dusty surface of a single facet of a diamond: a flat surface we crawl over as though that's all there is. When I let go of that "everyday," I become transparent. It's a reality that made me a stranger to myself. It's not that I've ever felt that something took "possession" of me, but rather that I became something I'd had no hint of before, inhabiting a mystery within which there are no directions. It's given me a tear-loosening awareness of beauty and how precious it is to the soul, and how plentifully available it is: every color, sound, sensation and natural form that is not of itself a source of some form of beauty....

SO ... what's a religion? It's certainly not what I see it commonly being claimed to be.

It's a mistake for outsiders to assume that religious people are necessarily virtuous. They're just people trying to draw meaning into their lives, much as hungry people look for food. Usually it's because of religions' transformative power that people are drawn to them. Some are just looking for company. At the same time, charlatans have always been eager to infiltrate and appropriate religions, and demagogues try to turn them to their own ends—and, when a charlatan dines with a demagogue, you can expect "forty days and forty nights" of sheer hell to ensue.

For much the same reason, religions attract the overly credulous. So, just as we've seen wars fought for "freedom," "peace," "democracy," "honor," "justice," "king and country," "manifest destiny," "civilization," "self-defence" and "the Empire," we've seen well-intentioned young soldiers led to slaughter in the name of a "god" hardly anyone knows anything about ... and where greed and hegemony have been the true but less banner-worthy causes.

Religions do offer teachings about personal conduct, whether it's being considerate towards other people or fasting, or abstaining from sex before a hunt. But mostly it's about focus: ways to avoid or limit distractions from the transformations that faith engenders. So it doesn't follow that everyone on the bandwagon is a kindly person or a good hunter. Many are needful, some are bullies, some are unbelievably kind. Stereotypes don't work. Nor does it help to turn religious teachings into rigidly enforced rules.

It's hard for a religion to demonstrate the degrees of difference it has made in people's lives: those lives must first be lived. Even the number of a faith's adherents can be misleading. Supply and demand don't hang together in a religion the way they're supposed to in a business plan.

> *I've found that changing my spiritual course is more like steering a ship than a car. The front wheels of a car pull it abruptly into the turn. A ship steers from the stern: the turned rudder begins to move a ship around its pivot point, some way back from the bow, setting a number of forces into turmoil around the ship's hull and in the water nearby: pushing water away from the stern on the side opposite to the turn, and sucking water towards the hull on the other. Water's heavy, and the response to a ship's wheel is resisted. The rudder of a ship re-orients the whole vessel from the stern, then its propellers can drive it forward in the new direction. If a ship's rudder is turned too hard and too far, it simply slows the vessel down because the turbulence that's created on either side of the blade cancel each other out. Rudders these days are pivoted, not as close as possible to the hull, but with about a third of its area ahead of the axis around which it turns. This takes stresses off the post and rudder system and means the rudder can be smaller. Olden rudders in the days of sail were enormous—with matching forces of torque—and took tremendous exertion, often on the part of several sailors, to manage. Modern rudder design is complicated, varied and sophisticated. It's amazing to see the work that tugboats need to do to move a ship that's not being controlled by its own rudder system. On a big ship, the wheel seems unresponsive*

at first but, if it's then turned harder to bring the ship around, it will produce too prolonged a turn and that, in turn, will need to be corrected. And a ship still moves forward on its old course as it turns. Turns at sea take time and care. Charts are important, and experience helps.

9
Sources ... e.g., Christianity

THE PORZIUNCOLA: A SMALL CHURCH THOUGHT TO HAVE BEEN RESTORED BY ST. FRANCIS, AND WHERE THE FRANCISCAN MOVEMENT BEGAN. IT IS NOW ENCLOSED WITHIN THE BASILICA OF SANTA MARIA DEGLI ANGELI NEAR ASSISI, ITALIA.

CHRISTIANITY's core (but far from only) source has long been the four "canonical" Gospels: Matthew, Mark, Luke and John. They launch the New Testament, which roughly accounts for the last quarter of the Holy Bible.‡ The first three quarters of the Bible are background and introductory stuff, lifted from sacred Jewish sources to set the context that launched the movement we've come to call "Christianity."

Scores of gospels were written: Robert Price's *The Pre-Nicene New Testament* (2006) includes 54 of them.[60] Some of them are pretty disappointing, others are known to have been lost and a few more may yet turn up. But, not least because

---

‡ Oddly, one might think, the Bible that Christians use opens with what might be considered background notes that make up three-quarters of the book. This consists of extensive excerpts from Jewish scriptures, from the Torah, the historic books, the Septuagint and the prophets.

such documents had long been ignored, unknown or suppressed, it was in Price's book that nearly 30 documents from the first three centuries of Christianity were published for the first time. They included newly discovered texts and reconstructions of the Gospel of Marcion and the Gospel According to the Hebrews. They give a fascinating, widened picture of what the Christian hope excited among people of that time.

There was clearly a widening buzz about this spiritual movement 2,000 years ago, though nothing is known for sure about Jesus as a historical figure. Some scholars doubt that he ever existed, Robert Price having come to agree with them. If Jesus did exist, he'd have answered to "Yeshua": a common Hebrew name that aptly means "rescuer" or "liberator." And "Christ" isn't a surname: it's the Greek rendering of the Hebrew title "Messiah" with the meaning of one "anointed": a ruler.

Most scholars allow that there probably was a real person who seeded an oral tradition that became Christianity. If we allow that a popular movement sprang up around such a person—I see no reason not to—we can use the name "Jesus" (or "Liberator") as aptly as any other. And the posthumous title "Christ" works, at least as one of Jesus' many metaphorical identities. During his lifetime, he seems to have been known as Jesus "of Nazareth" or Jesus, "son of Joseph."

Anyway, this isn't history we're talking about. It's a set of spiritual teachings that challenged, subverted and, in the end, surpassed the supremacy of Imperial Rome ... and a few other empires as well, come to that.

If the Gospels seem needful of rational explanation, we're reading them the wrong way. They move from incident to incident in ways that draw a reader's emotions and spirituality into a roller-coaster journey of inexplicable hope to its realization in life's fulfillment: a progression that lies at the core of Christian faith. There's less explicit instruction than you might hope or expect, and more parable. Incidents typically follow a logic that frustrates snap interpretation and everyday assumptions. "Miracles," for example, are reminders that none of this is historical so much as transformative. Explanations unfold in spiritual rather than rational reflection.

The narrative flamboyance inspired by Christian faith reached its heights far later than the Gospels. Look, for example, at the medieval hagiographies of various saints: a genre of delight exemplified by writers like Jacobus de Voragine who, writing in the thirteenth century, embellished oral lore with fanciful explorations of the significance of his saints' names that elaborate their divine inspiration.[61] So, of Saint Remigius of Rheims who famously baptized Clovis, King of the Franks, on Christmas Day, 508, Jacobus wrote:

> *Remigius is said of "remi," that is to say feeding, and "geos," that is earth, as who saith feeding the earthly people with doctrine. Or of "geon," that is a wrestler, for he was a pastor and a wrestler, he fed his flock with the word of preaching, with suffrages of praying...."*

To modern minds, this is all a bit artless but some of the olden hyperbole still echoes in the present day. It was, for example, an incident recorded by the seventh-century Abbott of Iona, Adomnán of Iona, writing about the sixth-century Celtic Saint Columba,[62] that launched the legend of the Loch Ness monster. Bolstered by some seriously ambiguous recent sightings, "Nessie" stirs something in the imaginations of the thousands of tourists a year who head to Drumnadrochit's Loch Ness Centre. Sure, there's bunk and credulity in all of this but it makes a tidy contribution to Scotland's tourism industry. Objecting to it outright would be a wrongheaded judgment against the kinds of fascination that have shaped our culture and continue to shape it.

Buzzing our imaginations is what the entertainment industry's all about. We've seen George Lucas' 1977 science-fiction/fantasy movie *Star Wars* inspire an atheistic cult of self-proclaimed "Jedi." The Jedi Temple—a registered non-profit corporation based in Beaumont, Texas[63]—ordains ministers and has a creed that goes like this:

> *I am a Jedi, an instrument of peace; where there is hatred I shall bring love; where there is injury, pardon; where there is doubt, faith; where there is despair, hope; where there is darkness, light; and where there is sadness, joy. I am a Jedi. I shall never seek so much to be consoled as to console; to be understood as to understand; to be loved as to love; for it is in giving that we receive; it is in pardoning that we are pardoned; and it is in dying that we are born to eternal life. The Force is with me always, for I am a Jedi.*

Now that might rattle a few Christians who are familiar with the prayer and hymn *Make Me an Instrument of Your Peace*. The text (without the wee Jedi tweaks) has shadowy origins and has been wrongly attributed to St Francis of Assisi. But Mother Theresa of Calcutta and Desmond Tutu are among thousands of people who've acknowledged it as a source of inspiration. In January 1916, Pope Benedict XV had an Italian version of an earlier, possibly original, French version published on the front page of the Vatican's *L'Osservatore Romano* newspaper as a prayer for peace during the First World War.

AFTER the Gospels, the Bible gives readers the surviving and purported works of Saint Paul aka Saul. His letters are the oldest Christian writings we have.

He was a Jewish zealot, a Pharisee, with Roman citizenship, born in Tarsus. He got about. In his early days he delighted in rounding up and harassing Christians. Then, says the biblical account in the Acts of the Apostles, he freaked out:

"Now as he was going along and approaching Damascus, suddenly a light from heaven flashed around him. He fell to the ground and heard a voice saying to him, 'Saul, Saul, why do you persecute me?' He asked, 'Who are you, Lord?' The reply came, 'I am Jesus, whom you are persecuting. But get up and enter the city and you will be told what you are to do.' The men who were travelling with him stood speechless because they heard the voice but saw no-one."[64]

In a 1987 paper in the *Journal of Neurology, Neurosurgery, and Psychiatry*, Dr. David Landsborough III suggested that Saul might have been felled by an attack of temporal lobe epilepsy. The clinicians' diagnoses escalated. A few years later, Dr. John Bullock at Wright State University, Ohio, was wondering whether a lightning strike could not have done the trick. In 2015, in the journal *Meteroritics and Planetary Science*, William Hartmann of the Planetary Science Institute in Arizona suggested that Saul could have been the shaken survivor of an exploding meteor.

The Bible is less extravagant. It actually offers two somewhat conflicting accounts of the incident, which isn't really the point here. If it was just a case of sunstroke or fatigue, or an excited imagination, it wouldn't matter. What's startling is that Paul suddenly switched sides and began organizing, encouraging, networking and instructing scattered Christian communities in their faith. He visited, he wrote letters, he endured imprisonments, beatings, privations and harassment, all the while fearlessly proclaiming that his messages came from a Jesus he'd never met in person.

Something seems to be missing from the story. He'd have us believe that his conversion was sudden and dramatic. Yet his teaching was remarkably well-formed, aware, boldly authoritative and delivered with articulate self-confidence. Falling off a horse is an odd source for these sorts of proficiencies. Yet 14 of the 27 books of the *New Testament* have traditionally been attributed to him and they've been as influential in shaping Christendom as the Gospels. The depth and passion of these teachings echo with relevance to the present day. Half of them are reckoned by scholars to have genuinely been Paul's work.

They regularize, they set the scene for orthodoxy and for "church." Could the teachings they pass on, which pre-date the *Gospels*, have been inspired by the forbearance, faith and understandings he had seen among the un-named, unrecorded Christians he'd harassed?

FOR fun, as well as for its depiction of the human condition in the early days of what we've been taught to call "civilization," I've been reading Ovid's 12,000-line gods-wrangling poem *Metamorphoses*.

Here we find Jove trying oafishly to hide his rape of pretty Io from his wife, Juno, by turning the guiltless Io into a cow. Io's father, the river god Imachus, laments that he cannot end his grief by death: "it is a hurtful thing to be a god, for the gates of death are firmly closed against me." Juno knows everything anyway and has Io, still mooing, herded off to Egypt where she becomes the River Nile, worshipped as Isis by the Egyptians.

Here's the lust-maddened Phoebus, demigod son of Jove, running down the beautiful Daphne who begs her father's protection. So her dad, Peneus, turns her into a laurel tree. Phoebus' lust hasn't quite cooled; he denies his shame by telling her that triumphant generals will wear her leaves on their brows, just as he will use it to decorate his own hair, lyre and arrow quiver. And here's Syrinx spurning lascivious Pan. She escapes by leading him to believe she's turned into reeds. He, still simmering with desire, pulls up a reed, finds its hidden music and fashions the world's first "Pan pipes." Here too is the musical Orpheus and his death-defying love of Eurydice. The stories are blunt but insightful. Their imagery engagingly intertwines and sets its own stage; their themes express an amoral but intelligible logic.

Ovid's moral insouciance—he was into his third marriage by the time he was 30, and his extended poem *Ars Amatoria* was a naked, full-frontal manual of seduction—got him exiled by the prim and austere Emperor Augustus. Ovid's amorality was that of the Second Triumvirate that Augustus had just supplanted. Divorce rates were high, infidelity was a norm; class, wealth and power stratified public life. Life could be extravagant, for a few, or brutally desperate.

Metamorphoses is a vivid excursion into the spirit world that was shaped by classical Greco-Roman mythology, a decade or two before the rise of Christianity. The point is that Ovid's vain, quarrelsome and petulantly lustful gods are born anew in each human generation. They personify the impulses that animate our inner wildernesses. We know them and we fear them. They're the enslaving elements of human psychopathology and we face terrible needs for the constraints of social morality to curb our capacities for cruelty.

Legislation won't contain it. We're merely human. The old gods' immortality and power gives them an innocent incomprehension of our suffering: they exist to please themselves and nothing stands in their way. We are their playthings. They murder, torture, rape and exact revenge for real or apparent slights—or simply because they feel like it. But their fate is worse ours: they are stricken with immortality.

IT's all a mirror.

The radicalism of early Christianity's new teachings must have been startling in psychological and spiritual contexts like these. A call to stand "with" god would have been as unnerving in the domain of the demigod Caesar Augustus as it seems to many "modern" folk today. And the idea of god becoming mortal? That's even further off the wall.

> SANTO DOMINGO 2015:
> *The glass is broken: splintered*
> *around the decrepit cenotaphs*
> *of fiends who broke the souls*
> *... their genocide, their ravishments,*
> *their enslavings and invadings*
> *that launched the long Kristallnacht*

of the Caribbean.
The sewage-stung sea
sobs for what is taken:
so all are commemorated
and somehow
they get by, the heirs of outrage:
the crumb gatherers
under the outer tables of
the dollared ones whose fathers
—priests and pirates—
join the old procession,
buying cheap and gaudy
souvenirs of reciprocal poverty:
trinkets to distance their souls
from alien truths ...
they get by.
They endure.

SO ... to the Christian narratives.

Susceptible as I am to satire, I'm drawn to the stories about Jesus' ride into Jerusalem during Passover. He jerked along on a donkey, spoofing the leaden pomp of Caesar's ordered cavalry and their entries into the Holy City. And, think about it: to parody an oppressor's public conceit takes chutzpah. But the story has other dimensions. It was a "triumph." It fulfilled a 500-year-old prophecy attributed to one of the twelve minor prophets, Zechariah: "Rejoice greatly, O daughter of Zion! Shout aloud, O daughter of Jerusalem! Lo, your king comes to you; triumphant and victorious is he, humble and riding on a donkey, on a colt, the foal of a donkey. He will cut off the chariot from Ephraim and the war-horse from Jerusalem; and the battle bow shall be cut off, and he shall command peace to the nations; his dominion will be from sea to sea and from the River to the ends of the earth."[65] And that's kind of funny too.

And all of this is about ways in which the early church saw itself. It announces what it thought its (and Jesus') purpose was. Had, for example, Jesus chosen to take on the mantle of the Messiah and play a political role in the emancipation of the Jews? Then why twit Caesar? Who supplied the donkey? How was that arranged? Did it happen at all? In the cultural context of the day, the donkey indicated peaceful intentions. So what was the message? And the next thing Jesus is reportedly doing is raising hell in the Temple?

These days, Palm Sunday commemorates the story. It is marked in various ways in different cultures and churches. Was the story an addition after Jesus' death, included to add credibility to the greater narrative by fulfilling ancient prophecy? Or were the Gospel writers teasing their novices with that prospect? There are no other independent references to the incident, but that does not diminish the narrative value of the Gospel accounts.

All of these questions are naïve, simply because they come from an alien, unfamiliar place. Gospel writers, driven by the crises and needs of their own time and place, chose texts for their relevance to their own situation, and their fruitfulness as teaching tools. Besides, the story of Jesus' entry to Jerusalem for the Passover "fits" the greater narrative in a way that enhances the significance and entirety of both.

Jesus' reported teachings and actions repeatedly teased, exposed and subverted the vacuity of core Roman tenets and the compromises of collaborationist Jewish Temple priests. And, to the extent that those betrayals of humanity remain in our world, Jesus' critique is no less sharp or immediate ... unless, like the Jewish mob, we chicken out. Or, like right-wing American fundamentalist literalists, turn it all on its head.

To "get" the Gospels, you really have to think, you have to engage. You won't find them consistent or reasonable; they're littered with contradictions and unanswered questions. But you may find them hypnotic, dream-inducing and touching strangely on your inner questions and feelings. They can be more apt than they first seem, and the meanings they hold unfold or pop into mind as they interact with the varieties of experience our lives hold.

The Gospel stories are teaching tales—not biography, not reportage, not history—from an oral tradition. They address you as an individual. Oral culture transmits itself through stories like these, in imagery and often in partnership with music, art and ritual. Variations in the tone and contexts of telling freshen insights that draw people into closer community. Oral narrative insists on participation. It's not "head stuff"; it's about "be-ing" and doing. So, for example, the words unique to the Gospel of John—"I give you a new commandment: that you love one another. Just as I have loved you, you also should love one another. By this everyone will know that you are my disciples. If you have love for one another"[66]—can be seamlessly attributed to Jesus, regardless of whether he ever said it exactly that way.

Jesus—our lead character in all of this, whether real or fictional—was clearly literate, but chose not to commit his teachings to writing. I suspect he (or his chroniclers) saw more worth in the pliant discernment of oral tradition and the participatory engagement of his followers than in the distancing intellectualism of Roman and Greek scholarship. Nor would the complex, traditions-laden language of Jewish scripture have served the need. But, as oral tradition, engaging directly with experience day to day, Jesus' teachings would gather meaning and, like rising bread, stay fresh and lively, challenging and inspiring. At the core of this process, in symbolic opposition to Roman eagles, Jesus placed an intimate ritual feast of bread and wine in remembrances of himself and his teachings.

This has the hallmark not of a legalistic "religion" but of a movement.

Oral narratives, bouncing around in a community, grow in relevance, diverge in detail and concentrate or dilute potency. As they reach more and more people, they assimilate sub-stories and circumstantial color; they omit what's overly obscure, confusing or particular to exceptional times. As a result, they can remain vivid long after the demise of their sources.

SO what happened? Why were so many "gospels" locked up in writing? Had Paul converted Christianity to literacy? Written down, the narratives lose the vitality, dynamism and inclusiveness of debate and discussion; documents resist group intelligence, collective experience, inquiry and imagination. They can inhibit questions rather than excite them. They risk freezing the freedom of being.

The writers of the *Gospels* are lost in shadows. What we see in their texts—those that survive—are vivid glimpses of the kinds of consciousness that sustained some of the earliest Christian communities. They are short documents, the longest (Luke) having fewer than 20,000 words. They're colored by contemporary experience and the poetic impulses of teachers and scribes.

Looking at other oral traditions, you'll find core cultural wisdom withheld from outsiders and transcribers. Transcription happened only when life got precarious. I think of Elsdon Best in New Zealand who published energetically about Maori culture in the late nineteenth and early twentieth centuries, albeit from a highly Eurocentric perspective. And Te Rangi Hiroa (Sir Peter Buck), whose landmark ethnographic works[67] were published in the 1930s and '40s. These emerged at a time when many doubted whether Maori culture would, could or should survive.

Imperiled cultures around the world have done the same. In *The Falling Sky*, Yanomami shaman Davi Kopenawa entrusts his Amazonian tribe's shamanic lore to print explicitly to avoid its being lost forever.[68] Ishi, the lone survivor of the Yahi tribe of California, emerged from the woods in 1911 and moved into a university museum in San Francisco to spend the last five years of his life helping anthropologists record his people's historical existence and culture. So ... what about the early Christians whose earliest Gospels date from late in the first century?

THE ROMANS excelled at erasing obstinate opposition, right down to the rootstock. The ruins of Carthage and Corinth attested to their ruthlessness.

So, in the year 70, every Jew in the Roman Empire and beyond must have been shaken to the quick as accounts reached them of the Roman legions' sacking of Jerusalem and the slaughter or enslavement of its citizens, the massacre of thousands of well-to-do Jews in Damascus, the razing of the Second Temple, the horrific fall of Masada, and, between 132 and 136, the disastrous Bar Kokhba revolt. Emperor Hadrian set out to extirpate Judaism, banning Torah law and having Jewish scholars executed. The Sacred Scroll was publicly burned; Judea was renamed "Syria Palestina." Jews were expelled and Jerusalem was re-named "Aelia Capitolina."

Why? Because Rome could ... and because the Jews had become to Rome what al Qaeda would become to George Bush. It's easy to think, in such a world, that whatever's not written down is in peril.

Enter eschatological Christianity. Instead of "judge not," "forgive," injunctions against not storing up treasures on earth—"for where your treasure is, there your heart will be also"[69]—and assurances of "god's kingdom" among us, expect the end of time, judgment and cataclysm. So about one-third of the synoptic Gospels came to focus on Jesus' last days.

John of Patmos' distress resulted in his Book of Revelation. The first word he wrote down was *apokalypsis*. In his Alexandrian Greek it just meant "revelation" but John sped it to the new meaning you'll find in the *Oxford Dictionary* of today: "an event involving destruction or damage on a catastrophic scale." To the banal cruelties of disease, conquest, famine and death he gave dark celebrity as its "Four Horsemen." These horrors had stalked the world long before the fall of Jerusalem, and dispense mass human misery to this day. But Jesus' hopes and intentions were clearly for something very different.

Less fevered followers of "The Way" (the original name of Christianity according to some sources), teachers and scribes, secured their only treasure by writing down the core of it all: the teaching stories ... our Gospels. Elaine Pagels tells us that "secret writings" from Nag Hammadi in Egypt encourage hearers to ask questions about Jesus' teachings and about the meanings of the scriptures, so "in the *Dialogue of the Saviour*, Mary Magdalene asks Jesus about his parable of the mustard seed and about certain sayings—'Today's trouble is enough for today' (*Matthew 6:34*)—before she receives new insight and speaks 'as a woman who has completely understood.'"[70]

Some saw the world's future lying among the peoples of the Roman Empire: the only ordered society where "civilization" might survive. After all, Acts recalls that it was Jews, not Romans, who stoned the Christian deacon Stephen to death, giving fledgling Christianity its first martyr.

Others were loath to surrender their Jewish roots.

Nero's first systematic campaign of extermination against Christians after the fire of Rome in the year 64 was followed by Domitian's ethnic cleansing aimed at Jews and Christians alike. Persecutions continued—here and there, on and off—until 361, by which time martyrdom had found a place in mainstream Christian consciousness and theology.

But longer-term dangers face written material.

The written word won't be understood in the way it was intended if read in contexts that are at odds with the one in which it was produced: shifted assumptions and different experiences lead to different conclusions.

And the world changed radically for Christians. In the fourth century, Emperor Constantine ("the Great") flipped. He ended the persecutions and launched Christianity's future as the official religion of Europe. Roman state authorization and an approved canon of sources were as deeply damaging as the persecutions. Constantine's act wasn't a surrender; it was more like a takeover.

The scene was set for the first big split in Christendom: the rift between Eastern Orthodoxy and (Western) Roman Catholicism. Roman Catholicism has spent 1,500 years coming to terms with its institutionalization, and still struggles.

The second big fracture—the Reformation in the sixteenth century—saw Protestantism embrace the social libertarianism of the Enlightenment and delight in the regicides that culminated in the extinction of the Romanovs. Religious impulse hardened into zealous moralism. All of this was at the expense of our capacities for faith, not because of the social improvements but because of the way the foundations of our conceptual universe were shifted.

Nowadays, few younger people spontaneously find the writings of Edmund Spenser, Chaucer, Langland and Shakespeare interesting, nor even intelligible: 500 years of social change has drop-kicked some of English literature's most culturally significant writing out of the park. Jesus' words found their resonance 1,500 years prior to Shakespeare and Spenser, and several cultures removed. It doesn't help Christians to be so awed by the Bible's significance that they swerve from thinking about that conceptual relocation. We lose the plot when we ignore the chasms.

Translations and the contexts in which Christianity is presented to the world can make matters worse. By way of contrast, though the Arab world has changed dramatically, the Holy Qur'an is still borne aloft by the vivacity and cultural dynamism of the Arabic language and its script. It has living referents and contexts to enliven its poetic essence.

SO, can the wealth of Jesus' ministry be resuscitated? Should it be?

A good way to explore both questions would be to re-learn the ways of listening that survive in primal cultures, starting among the too-widely despised native peoples of the "New World." As some pioneers of contextual theology (as opposed to systematic theology) are already attempting, we need hear the narratives personally and culturally.

This means letting the stories transform us. They were never intended to "persuade" us. The facts that might persuade a rational modern mind simply aren't there. It's a case not of searching in the wrong haystack, but of looking for the wrong needle.

Scripture's a wilderness that teases us towards meaning: meaning is implicit, not explicit. Historical narrative is something altogether else. History's a modern Western conceit. For too long, we've ignorantly, arrogantly and intolerably dismissed oral cultures as "pre-literate" and, therefore, "inferior" and, hence, lacking a worthwhile narrative. It's an attitude that long scorned as "accidental" the extraordinary voyages of early Polynesia's navigators and the achievements of canoe captains who planted new communities on every inhabitable island of the eastern Pacific. They transplanted crops and animals from South East Asia and South America back and forth across a vast commonwealth ... all of this before European navigators first ventured into the world's largest oceanic expanse.

I'd love to see a new Christian "mission" pick up the precedent of a few recent interfaith explorations within the United Church of Canada and venture further into the world—not to proselytize but to listen and learn and become a movement again. Jesus taught that there were many rooms in god's "house" ... and he wasn't talking about Baptists, Mormons or Seventh Day Adventists. Nothing in his teachings justifies the long-practiced impositions on others of narrow-minded theological and spiritual conquest by some "Christians." If we're going to be bothered with any of it, we need to heal our heads of the sickness that's based wholly and solely on morose factuality. It's as unhelpful as trying to understand our children by reading up on animal husbandry. And sometimes we simply need to get outdoors and play.

> When my wife, Sue, announced to me that she felt powerfully called to ministry in the bicultural Methodist Church of New Zealand—Te Haahi Weteriana o Aoteroa—I was worried. We weren't churchgoers. I was a journalist with a job I thoroughly enjoyed, and I could see an exciting future ahead. I was still alienated from the church in particular and "religion" in general. But I also dearly love my wife. So, to help orient myself to the idea, and possibly to find a way out, I spent quite a bit of time making a list of all the things I felt were "true" and "good"; principles and values I held dear. It was harder than I expected ... and my list? It was crap. I shamed myself. The stuff I "really, really" believed in was, when I "really, really" thought about it, shallow, effete and stupid. So, after some weeks of reflection, I told Sue: "Okay ... your bullshit looks better than my bullshit, so let's give it a shot and see where we end up." I would stay at home and look after our daughter, then a three-year-old, and support Sue as best I could while she went through her theological training. We were both unfamiliar with the way this stuff worked so, before we moved to Auckland and a tiny, seminary-provided apartment, we sold up what we had and gave the proceeds to "the poor," as Jesus said in the Bible. When we got to college, one of the first things they put in Sue's hand was a parking permit for the car we didn't have ... and the following four years of poverty were some of the best, most stimulating and enjoyable years of our lives, even for our little girl.

WHEN I began looking with a fresh eye and a more open mind at the Christian deal, Sue was training for ministry and pointed me to amazing stuff: feminist scholars like Schüssler Fiorenza, Mary Daly, Grace Jantzen and others who were leveling previously unchallenged theological blockhouses. I found treasuries of Christian mysticism I'd never heard of: Hadewijch of Antwerp, writing in the thirteenth century: fresh and startling even today. Hildegard of Bingen, Catherine of Siena, Julian of Norwich, Meister Eckhart ... and more recent figures like Thomas

Merton, Dietrich Bonhoeffer, Simone Weil and Matthew Fox all plunged into faith with vitality and courage. Through them, I began to get glimpses of Jesus' flair for finding harmonies: drawing faith, spiritual energy, raw life, god-awareness and knowledge together with transforming discernment.

Even 2,000 years of churchianity, of abuse, of ethnocentrism and bigotry, of self-justification and conceit, power-seeking and bullying, squabbling, fighting, greed, translation and interpretation, abuse, subversion, superstition, division, sectarianism, betrayal, bullshit and misappropriation have amazingly failed to destroy the kernel of truth at Christianity's core ... and that priceless kernel is what we owe to the redactive genius of Jesus. The rest is church- and people-baggage.

REDACTION? Jesus? To "get" that, I can't help thinking it'd be healthy and refreshing around now to acknowledge the essence of some of the ancient wisdom traditions that seemed to find their way into the mix: they lead us back towards the first people of the planet and the origins of human consciousness. They lead us across continents and across cultures. And, in knowing and learning from the ancient wisdom bearers of his day, Jesus could with complete integrity announce: "Very truly I tell you, before Abraham was, I am."[71]

It'd also be timely now, I believe, to explore the United Church of Canada's interfaith initiatives more deeply: we might well find spiritual healings for our society, our world and ourselves. Ovid's gods and our materialism are trashing all of us. Our search is an ever-ongoing one. That "the 'Son of Man' has no place to lay his head"[72] is a truism. Faith's a journey not a place. It's a movement, not an institution.

THE idea that Jesus was a redactor has no firm historic foundation. And the historical evidence that can be cobbled into a single actual-factual person called "Jesus" is worse than unhelpful: its flimsiness makes it a distraction. So just bear with me a bit.

Jesus' "influences" may not have been formalized or attributed by the Gospel writers, but it's inconceivable that they weren't in the air. The people of his time and place engaged with esoteric, mystical and philosophical ideas as vigorously as we bathe our sickening spirits in "news," entertainment and social media. Teachers, philosophers, cultists, shamans, seekers, crazies and seers roamed the Holy Land—and the Roman Empire—seeking, arguing about, and expounding "truths" and "wisdom." Jesus rose so far above the radar, so to speak, that the Romans thought it best to have done with him. Herod had already disposed of Jesus' provocative cousin, John.

I'm sure Jesus was crucified to show where the bar was set. It was a simple statement that you don't make waves in Jerusalem during Passover and expect to get away with it. But the Romans were too late—the "resurrection" was all too evident in the communities that were springing up here and there around their Eastern Empire. Teachings brought together in his name had animated a vigorous movement, no matter that it was scattered and inconsistent.

To shine in such times and company, as Jesus must have, was remarkable. I'm happy to call it a "holy miracle" if that's the language you want to use ... or "visionary brilliance".

Until Christianity, as far as I know, there was no spiritual or philosophical bridging on a comparable scale: rather, masses of insight were expressed in the confines of intellectual or arcane control that, in their own separate ways, made it all too structured, too exclusionary, too distant from lived experience.

I BEGAN my reflections around why Matthew 2:16 is the only clear Gospel reference to a "flight to Egypt"; Luke 2:39–40 says Jesus grew up in Nazareth, Galilee, and went with his parents to Jerusalem every year for the Passover festival. Anyway, Herod's infanticidal purge has no historical basis beyond Herod's personality profile.

Why the reference to Egypt?

In Jesus' day, Egypt was a leading centre of learning. The Museum of Alexandria and its library were famed. Rome had done the museum no favours, but it survived as a vital and well-resourced centre of scholarship and learning. Plato spent 13 years studying in Egypt, and there was an infusion of North African influence into Greek thought.

MAYBE, I thought, Matthew's reference to Egypt stemmed from apparent influences that his community spotted? Scholars, in their way, think that Matthew's Gospel probably originated in the Roman spa city of Heirapolis in Turkey, a place known for its bustling religious diversity. People there might have been expected to recognize parallels of thought.

Even in Nazareth, Jesus could well have had access to an abundance of Greek and Egyptian ideas. Perhaps that's why, in the Luke story, the 12-year-old Jesus was able to so precociously impress the Temple priests that Passover. Maybe Matthew and Luke just had different ways of making the same claim.

Jesus would urge, for example, the supremacy of love over the law. The Egyptian concept of Ma'at institutionalized something similar. When the law was an ass, its victim could appeal to Ma'at: a unified principle of truth, fineness of balance, morality, justice and order.

Ma'at was personified as a goddess whose purview was the stars, the seasons and the order of the universe. She stood for a desirable fineness of balance and exactitude that was considered the norm for nature and society, in this world and the next. Hers was the spirit in which justice should be applied, rather than detailed legalistic exposition. We could use a Ma'at-based High Court of Appeal in our day, age and culture. Ma'at was herself in balance with Isfet, the principle of chaos, injustice and disorder.

ANYWAY, the Holy Land under Roman rule was anything but isolated. And, within reason, all sorts of gods and philosophies were tolerated. The Pax Romana was all about promoting trade, and trade meant traders and travellers and, more in those days than now, a lot of face-to-face cross-cultural exchange. So, even if Jesus never went to Egypt, it's a safe bet that he'd have had plenty of opportunities to meet educated Latin or Greek-speaking Egyptians.

In the same way that Ma'at seems to be echoed in the teachings of Jesus that have come to us 2,000 years later, other influences from other faiths are suggested.

SILK may have been the glamor trade item from China; paper was more important than silk. But the Old Silk Road was not just a direct conduit for goods from Asia to Roman Europe. Goods passed through networks and intermediaries across the Asian continent. So the West, for example, owes something of its enjoyment of apples to caravaneers of the Old Silk Road.

But, most significantly, it carried ideas, religions, artistic influences, technologies, knowledge, philosophies, social influences and insights. Scholars have traced the movement—east and west—of Persian Zoroastrianism, Buddhism, Judaism and other early religions and cultural traditions along the routes of the Silk Road. One documented fusion is the existence of Greco-Buddhist art. Many have credited trade on the Old Silk Road with influences on civilizations along its entire route: China, South Asia, Persia, the Middle East and Europe.

Jerusalem in Jesus' day was not homogenously and singularly Jewish. And Damascus, a wealthy western terminus along the Silk Road, was "just up the road." For anyone who went looking, the Holy Land must have been staggeringly ideas-rich and spiritually energized. And Jesus, I can only imagine, was the sort of young man who'd go looking.

It was along the Old Silk Road that Buddhism launched the first big missionary movement in the known history of world religions. Roman accounts describe a Buddhist embassy to Caesar Augustus sometime between 22 B.C. and 13 A.D. It carried a diplomatic letter written in Greek. The writer Will Durant suggested in the 1930s that this mission might have helped to lay the ground for Christian teaching.

But there was more to it than that. Merchants found Buddhism appealing and supported the Buddhist monasteries along their trade routes. The monasteries hosted merchants along the way and some of the communities formed this way grew into organized centres of literacy and culture.

THE Chinese philosopher Mozi lived 400 years before Jesus. His following was in decline by Jesus' time but not extinct. Like Jesus' dad, Mozi was a carpenter. He was, in fact, something of an early Chinese Leonardo da Vinci. He invented all sorts of devices, from mechanical birds to mobile "cloud ladders," to attack city walls. And he designed defences. He was known as a strategist and architect, hired by warlords as a military advisor.

He'd hoped to replace the Chinese attachment to family with "universal love" ("Jian'ai": 兼愛), arguing that people should care for all people equally: "loving" one's enemies and caring for them was the only sure path to peace, he'd concluded. It sounds a bit like Jesus' reported teaching.

For a time, Mozi's teachings rivaled those of Confucius. Confucianism, Mozi felt, was too fatalistic, and promoted overly lavish celebrations and funerals that eroded the wellbeing and productivity of common folk.[73] Does that have an echo in Jesus' teaching, for example, that "the Sabbath was made for man, not man for the Sabbath"?[74]

The "attachment to family" issue turns up quite specifically in the Bible, in Matthew's Gospel: "While he (Jesus) was still speaking to the crowds, his mother and his brothers were standing outside, wanting to speak to him. Someone told him, 'Look, your mother and your brothers are standing outside, wanting to speak to you.' But to the one who had told him this, Jesus replied, 'Who is my mother, and who are my brothers?' And pointing to his disciples, he said, 'Here are my mother and my brothers! For whoever does the will of my Father in heaven is my brother and sister and mother.'"[75]

Mozi emphasized self-reflection and authenticity over obedience to ritual ... rather as Jesus later would. He encouraged people to lead lives of self-restraint, renouncing material and spiritual extravagance ... rather as Jesus later would. His passion was said to have been for the good of the people, without concern for personal gain or even his own life or death ... as Jesus later would.

Mozi fascinates me. His pragmatic rationale for universal love is obvious, but it has always offended power-seeking minds, and appalls human impulses to huddle around fires of immediate self-interest.

If I think of "universal love" as an example, I see Jesus reasonably trying to insinuate the insight into Jewish thought, and into wider, universal awareness. The whole direction of Jesus' teachings was not to conversion and homogeneity but to expansiveness and inclusion... that was his "way," his "truth" and his "life."

THROUGHOUT a vast area, the old Persian Achaemenid Empire had laid a basis of monotheistic Zoroastrianism. It's been estimated that in 480 BC, some 50 million people lived in the Achaemenid Empire: about 44 per cent of the world's population at the time. Its language, Aramaic, was the language of Jesus and used widely along the Old Silk Road.

The Israelites had long been Persia's captives—"*by the rivers of Babylon ...*"— and Zoroastrian influences found their way, as might be expected, into early Judaism.

Herodotus recorded that: "the most disgraceful thing in the world [the Persians] think, is to tell a lie; the next worst, to owe a debt: because, among other reasons, the debtor is obliged to tell lies."[76]

In Zoroastrianism, water and fire are agents of ritual purity, and the associated purification ceremonies are considered the basis of ritual life. Baptism was a Zoroastrian ritual; it became a Jewish one. In Zoroastrianism, life's a temporary state in which a mortal is expected to actively participate in the continuing battle between truth and falsehood. (Isn't that more or less a "scientific" view?)

THEN there was the Roman military cult of Mithraism, at its peak in Jesus' time. It was a mystery cult that's said to have taught that three wise men of Persia visited the baby savior-god Mithras, born on December 25, bringing with them gifts of gold, myrrh and frankincense. Some say the Romans' Mithras died on a cross, celebrated a "Last Supper" with his twelve disciples (who represented the twelve signs of the zodiac) and rose at the spring equinox. Where there are parallels in the Gospel accounts of Jesus' life, I'm inclined to see something like a game of spiritual "Snap" having gone on in the early communities: in Matthew's Jewish-Christian community, for example, which was probably in Roman-governed Syria ... especially when it comes to the birth narratives.

Meanwhile, Celts were talking with Greeks and Persians were meeting Vedantists and Jains (followers of one of the world's oldest known religions) along the Old Silk Road.

THE extent of my argument is not that Jesus or the early Christians poached ideas from other wisdom traditions and re-branded them as Jesus' own, but that they could not have been isolated from a heady mix of insight, wisdom, and philosophical understandings, including all sorts of non-Jewish religious interpolations. And their impulses may not have been too different from those of some eighteenth- and nineteenth-century Christian missionaries who drew parallels with the mythologies of alien cultures to make connections and initiate discussion towards conversion.

Saint Augustine of Hippo in the fourth century declared that "that which is called the Christian religion existed among the Ancients, and never did not exist, from the beginning of the human race until Christ came in the flesh, at which time the true religion, which already existed, began to be called Christianity."[77]

It's an observation that does nothing to detract from "Jesus," the faith called "Christianity," or the power of its substance. To my way of thinking, it helps to substantiate the soundness of Christianity's foundations, if not all that it's become. Those older, wider streams gave the original communities that took up the Jesus "way" a compelling context for the essence of their "truth" and greater hope for its preservation.

Direct, hard evidence of Jesus and what he taught?

That depends on a reading back from the hope that's expressed in the Gospels: certainly the antithesis of Roman pursuits of grandeur, wealth and power. History can lead us no closer to whatever interactions actually took place. There are no forensic tests to satisfy the questions we might want to raise. However, we can feel tantalized, and that tantalization is something I personally find faith-feeding.

My reading is that, along with teachings that challenge our society to the quick, the Gospels incite us to question, to think and to engage ... to love. And give us amazing tools to do it with.

THE Jesus persona seems to have had a special regard for the truths of bread and wine, quite apart from the "Last Supper" narrative. Within a group like Jesus' inner circle that seems to have often shared bread and wine and bandied about insights of faith, there are sound reasons to honor the dynamic.

We do something of the sort today when we find time to eat and drink together with our friends. I love preparing and sharing food. Shared meals un-cage conversations that are leisurely, trusting and deep enough to draw fresh insights into the light, and new ways to see life. Cooking and presenting food is an art that can express welcome, love, affection, reunion, respect and fun.

Jesus' considerable gift lay in his integration of all he encountered. His Jewish enculturation was a source of strength and inspiration, not a set of limiting preconceptions. Judaism was in a mess anyway, thanks to the Temple's need to appease a brutal occupying power. But it possessed enormous spiritual wealth, rooted in inherited narratives and a tradition of constant re-examination and re-interpretation ... one that goes on to this day.

Not least it inspired resistance to oppression.

THE big flaw in Christianity lies not in the teachings of Jesus but in some of the infrastructures it seeded: fortresses of belief, fear and legalism that warp Jesus' teachings to their antitheses. Still, we need instruction, we need practices, we need rituals and we need touchstones. But we need them for liberty, not for confinement. And we need them, first and foremost, for discernment.

I've come to see Jesus having vital relevance to us now ... in seeds sown and seeds blown that have yet to be brought to fruition. And I see this too in the Gospels: an underlying stream of assimilation and discernment, openness and wisdom. Drinking at this river does not need any more historical or rational justification than sharing a meal together ... than our capacity to find faith-energizing harmonies with others and with the world we inhabit. We can do it. We can experience it. We can become it. And we don't have to abandon our intellects to get there.

IN Christendom, since the vicious conflicts of the Reformation, throughout the Enlightenment and into the present day, religion has been widely propagandized against. It has fragmented. It is suspect. But, despite their legalism and some very dodgy bedfellows, their spiritual momentum has carried them through. They've survived the collapse of failed states. But they do carry the scars.

The Church is collapsing, states are failing, the economy is bursting at its seams.

Humanity is suffering, confused, abused and widely oppressed. Why should hope be so meagerly distributed, why should fear be offhandedly tolerated?

Faith, I have to assert, doesn't imply credulity. It simply needs to strengthen, as belief needs to wane.

This is simply spiritual good sense: broad-brush stuff, like breathing: I don't breathe to sustain my metabolic system. I breathe because I feel the need to.

Rivers of wisdom?

Same deal.

10
Why Not?

RAIL BRIDGE, TRENT RIVER, ONTARIO

MAYBE the question needs to be, "Why bother?"

Analogies like bread and wine leap to mind, but I'd need to drag them out from under some heavy stones, scrape off the layers of distancing that blunt olden pleasures and sustenance, and peel away a lot of boring supermarket dross.

I hold Otto Rohwedder partly to blame. An itinerant Iowan jeweler, he set up the world's first bread-slicing machinery in a bakery in Chillicothe, Missouri, in 1928. To show for it, we now have plastic bags of characterless dead dough. Nor will I let Thomas William Carlyon Angove off the hook: he's the Aussie chancer who started selling wine in plastic-lined cardboard boxes. Then there's the mad, marketing-driven New World wine boom that's led to wine being made faster, in vaster volumes and with more guzzle appeal.

Yes, "bread" and "wine" have both slid into pudgy mires of casual, careless consumption. And, when it comes to food and drink, concerns about convenience, allergies, calories, additives, fads and toxins have widely come to outweigh flavor, freshness and variety.

> ITALY: A good friend—a musician and instrument maker from Scotland—and I were sitting in a square in Barga, Tuscany. We were sharing bread and local spring water. It was 'real' bread, mixed and kneaded by hand. It had that extra quality that takes artistry as well as skill: a buoyant, yeasty lift, a chewy crust, and a sweet, reverberating array of satisfying wheaten flavors. Such bread gives me a wonderful feeling—a glow—of wellbeing. The water was cool, delicious and cleanly sweet, clearing the palate for a return of the bread's full flavor. We decided that, with such bread and such water, a bread and water diet mightn't be as cruel a hardship as we usually imagine. Then the wine came: a plain, local rosso in a thick, sun-warmed glass carafe. It was a wine that rolled out flavors from soil, air, fruit and skill... it enhanced the flavor of the bread even more than the water. Bread and water? Make that bread and wine ... this bread, this wine.

FOOD production and distribution have become formidably slick processes. But Sue, my partner in love, life and faith, is a gardener; I'm an appreciative cook. So, between us, we've made whole meals from a handful or two of crisp green beans picked from the vines that climb our patio. Lightly boiled, dusted with Parmesan and tossed with some freshly torn basil they bring us joy. Simplicity makes it sacred ... but so does its intimacy. We saw the seeds sprout, the flowers open, grow and fill out, and felt grateful when they've survived a storm or an unseasonal frost. We've delighted in their blooming and watched the bees collect their nectar. The basil is thick at our feet. In all of these little, local, nearby things there's a kind of grandeur.

I find the same sorts of pleasure in making bread. There's the aroma of the yeast proofing, the dusty feel of flour on my hands ... then the working, kneading and pressing of life into the dough that, instead of clinging to my fingers, starts clinging warmly to itself and becomes a pliant, resilient, clearly living whole. That sensual, warm responsiveness echoes and draws out delights we can recognize within ourselves.

Similarly, few pleasures draw me closer to appreciations of mystery than picking berries: there's something so compact, so intense and so repetitively pleasing about plucking one ripe berry after another. The fit they find with our longings can be explained in scientific terms, but that's not the kind of understanding that matters: it's the experience of that exquisite correspondence that cradles the wonderment.

Here in Canada, it's raspberries and blueberries; in Scotland, it was brambles. We called them "blackberries" in New Zealand, and cooked them with apples to eat with ice cream. My parents had a big, untidy garden and, running through everything, were passionfruit vines and "Cape Gooseberry" bushes (*Physallis peruviana*, or "ground cherries").

We'd scratch each other's names on green passionfruit with a nail and they'd come up white on the ripe, dark purple fruit. I courted girlfriends by writing their names on them, hoping we'd still be friends when the fruit, the sweetest aphrodisiac I know, finally ripened. If we'd broken up, I always felt better after eating their earmarked fruit myself. And, on lazy summer days, the Cape gooseberries would be all about, golden-sweet in their fragile husks, and pop delectably in my mouth.

> *It's better than being young again*
> *to mouth whole handfuls*
> *of fine black brambles,*
> *startle the cow from her shade,*
> *and send the rabbit bounding*
> *from her daybed;*
> *to burn at the nettle's touch*
> *and gnaw the bramble barb*
> *from the butt of my hand—*
> *To be stained purple this way,*
> *fill shelves with jars of berry jam*
> *and be warmed by the Cumbrae sun.*

AT times, we've had chickens around, gathered their eggs in the coolness of sparkling mornings to eat fresh, poached, for breakfast before setting off for the day. We've experienced raising, killing and eating our own chickens and geese. And I've helped a neighbor to kill and dress sheep. I've killed and eaten sea fish and fresh water fish. This is all tougher stuff than fruit and berries but it should never be too easy. Food's an intimate substance, a gift. Taking an animal's life is shocking and humbling. Losing sight of food's sources can make it all seem almost homogenous, its origins unfathomable. When that happens, as we've seen, circles of dependency are easily broken and leave us—or others—wastefully, negligently destitute. The necessary link comes back to narrative, to meaning.

> *REKOHU: The newspaper I worked for had sent me and a photographer to the Chatham Islands, a remote, lightly populated New Zealand territory on the edge of the Southern Ocean. These islands harbor breeding grounds for many of the region's seabirds. We'd been out working all day and hiked some good few miles when we got back to the small community where we'd rented a room. Tired and hungry, we found that the only place open was the pub. We asked at the bar what food they had. Bags of dry, salted, crisp stuff*

didn't appeal so we ordered beers. It wasn't long until a big, square-framed Maori guy came over to where we were sitting. "You hungry?" he asked. We told him where we'd been and that we hadn't got around to eating yet. "Bring your beers," he said and led us across the road to an old flatbed truck loaded with stacks of sack-covered crates. He pulled one of the boxes down and spilled a dozen or more big, spiny sea urchins—kina—onto the tray. With his knife, he began splitting them open. He spilled the dark entrails on the ground and offered us the part-shells with their golden-orange, finger-fat segments of sweet, salty roe. The worn, bleached-grey, boards of the truck-tray were our table, before us was the vivid, darkening sweep of Petre Bay and, beyond the bay, the vastness of ocean under a sunset-soaked sky. The shore, not 10 meters away, whispered the low-pitched hiss of slow swells as they rose then withdrew from the beach. The flavors of kina and beer mingled with the clean tang of sea-smells, and we three fell into a seamless, perfect, ocean-borne silence... the luminous grace of hospitality.

IT'S in first-hand experiences that I've found human capacities most persuasively open into those moments of self-blurring completeness. It happens through music; it happens in art ... it is a natural phenomenon that happens when we walk in wilderness or hazard the ocean ... it happens most powerfully when we give ourselves to love. Or open to what's immediately at hand.

It can happen pretty much wherever we let it and whenever we open to its being the ground we're walking on. It's not rationed. Life is good. To be miserable, life has to be reduced to misery. Does it matter? Does it change anything?

Engagement, kindness, acceptance and trust make life worthwhile. Even disappointment, grief and pain, as well as that richness of life, are made more, and more fully, accessible. These emotions work for us best when they are in balance. If we fear and avoid a part of that spectrum, we die a little in our heart of hearts. Opening to it all gives us a dignity of being, living for humanity's sake as well as for ourselves, more worthwhile.

It's not about doing stuff; it's about a way of being.

AOTEAROA: An elderly Samoan man, known in his home village as an expert canoe builder, traditional sailor and fisherman, sensing he would soon die, came to New Zealand to carve a single-person fishing canoe, a traditional paopao, for his son who was, and remains, a friend of mine. He first approached the local Maori people for a tree which, with ceremonies of gratitude and deference, was cut, trimmed, and drawn from the forest. The old man would not let a power tool near the trunk, but set patiently to work with adze and axe to form and hollow out the hull. It was time-consuming work, and he took the time it needed. I watched him chip away at the inside of the hull, leaving wood thick and strong enough to take the buffeting of hard use yet thin enough to endow the craft with speed, lightness, ease of handling and a shallow draft. He worked at it for hours on end with one hand pressed against the outside of the hull as he chipped away at the inside. He was feeling for the optimal thickness, taking into account variations in the density and grain of the wood. The thudding of the adze blows was as regular as a heart-beat.

I realized that he was lost in a dialogue with the tree: in his head and heart, there existed the perfect canoe, shaped by his years of experience; before him was an imperfect log: a particular tree trunk shaped by its life in the forest. There was only one possible canoe. And it could exist only for his son. No-one would be able to buy it or steal it without its losing its meaning. Similarly, there was no place for tape measures, set squares, saws or plans... the old man's lifetime of experience was finding its harmonies with the tree's existence and with the love he held for his son. Later, after the old man's canoe was launched and he had returned to Samoa, I had the privilege of riding in the canoe. I experienced its buoyancy-of-being: a buoyancy constructed of so many things.

THERE'S an art to crafting that buoyancy; it comes from within and it cries out to be shared.

ITALY: In the Italian Apennines, in northern Molise, is a pretty, orange-tiled hilltop village called Scapoli. It's at the centre of a revival of Southern Italy's traditional bagpipe, the zampogna. A dear friend in nearby Isernia drove me up the steep, winding road to experience the bagpiping festival held there each July. When we arrived, Scapoli's own pipers were out in their dark, knee-length cloaks, red ribbons and black felt hats, processing through the gathering crowds. With them went singers, accordion players and percussionists ... drums, cymbals, tambourines, castanets, grunting friction drums and clattering triccheballacche (a kind of triple-hammered clapper with metal rattles attached). And all around were seldom-seen bagpipes: baghets, musas and pivas from northern Italy, zampognas from Sicily and the south, bots from the Pyrenees, Highland Scottish and Irish pipes, gaitas and gaidas, dudas, sacs de gemecs from Spain and other instruments from around Europe. And there were sensuous, startling tarantella dancers from Sicily, singers, guitarists and other performers. Dancers took to the stages and performed, impromptu, in the street. The festival also holds a program of seminars, workshops, concerts and presentations. But, apart from the arranged events, musicians spend much of their time playing in the crowded streets, comparing instruments and repertoire with other musicians, or simply enjoying themselves and the music that crowds the air. A few stalls displayed piping supplies, crafts and souvenirs; others served porchetta, bread, smoked meats, conserves, cheeses ... a single Euro got you a slice of pizza nothing like the slimily layered vileness that's too often served as "pizza" in other countries ... while glasses of tasty local wine were costing half a Euro. Trestle tables and chairs drew visitors and performers. It was at such a sunlit table, with wine and food passed around, that I saw an elderly local instrument maker, a young woman piper from Scandinavia, a burly Serb, a costumed Spaniard, another Balkan piper I was told was a Croat, and several north Italian piva players locked in an animated multilingual discussion about their music and their instruments. Drones were being taken apart, reeds were being passed around, snatches of tune were being sung, chanter fingerings were being compared and shared, and the table rocked with laughter. This was the summer of 2002. Less than a year had passed since terrorist attacks felled New York's "twin towers"; the former president of Yugoslavia, Slobodan Milosevic, was being tried in The Hague for war crimes; United Nations weapons inspectors were futilely looking for evidence of "weapons of mass destruction" in an Iraq that was still ruled by Saddam Hussein. Serbs and Croats were simmering with the revival of old hatreds. And, from time to time, NATO military aircraft made snarling passes over the region. On the ground, in striking contrast, Scapoli had brought the whole of Europe laughing and sharing, to a single table.

EXPERIENCES like these—of a delight that's bigger than the sum of immediate interactions—are experiences of a potential. They implant hope and sensations of moral aptness. There's a word for it: "transcendence". It's a state of awareness that doesn't need a special mat, a posture or solitary silence. It's simply a shift out of self-preoccupation into a moment of deeper being. Such moments are never far away, if we're open to them. And, as we open to them, time and again, it gets easier. Life gets easier. Fear backs off and empathy shifts our being. Existence feels a better fit. We're helped to bend, to accept and share, to stretch and fit into life. Fitting in is about letting go, about giving rather than getting, about be-ing more than do-ing. We discover we aren't "owned" and we "own" nothing. Another's pain or plight becomes vivid to us and it's easier to stand beside that person.

> SCOTLAND: To use the washrooms at Glasgow's Queen Street Train Station you have to put a 20p coin in a slot to turn the turnstile. It was late afternoon and there was a line-up. Ahead of me was a lean young guy in a grey tee and old denims. I'd bought a Big Issue magazine from him a few hours before and told him to keep the change. The magazine is a charity: an advocate for homeless people and its street sellers who, working on a small commission, are all drawn from their ranks. Ahead of him, with a smart haircut, dark pinstripe suit, shiny black shoes and a laptop case, was someone I took to be a junior lawyer, or a newly-minted accountant. As we shuffled steadily closer to the clicking turnstile, this man was doing the "gotta-pee" two-step and digging through his pockets, passing his laptop from one armpit to the other, and looking more and more agitated. The Big Issue guy happened to turn and caught my eye. We grinned, having cruelly caught on that the suit-dude was short of a 20p coin. He reached the turnstile on the point of exploding into tears and collapsing into a widening yellow puddle on the pavement. The queue stopped moving. Big Issue guy turned and grinned again ... then, in the moment that took hold, he reached out and dropped a 20p coin in the slot. I last saw suit-dude half-running, laughing and hopping backwards as he thanked Big Issue guy. Big Issue guy put another 20p in the slot, walked through himself and gave me a grin ... 20p to make the three of us, passing strangers, laugh? That's not a bad deal.

WHEN the flawed realities confronting us overlap with others' worlds, we can be drawn into an awareness human of one-ness, a buoyancy of being. The Maori of Aotearoa have a word for that caring unity: *arohanui*: literally "big love," a kind of widely shared bonding, unity and uplift. Affinities and concern animate these connections, and there's an art to coming by them: like that of the old canoe builder, assimilating his hope and dream from his culture's essence, his embeddedness in its long ocean-going experience, his place within his family and his appreciation of the tree.

Healthy hopes and aspirations can't be bought. Nor can they be shaped in a day, nor by any quick fix. Life's not that easy, assertive or solitary. It takes a lot of listening, risk, openness, sensitivity and submission.

Along with that, most of the people I've met have experienced finding themselves in places beyond "knowing": mindscapes where we simply feel ... and wonder. For simplicity's sake, let's call this arousal of awe an experience of "holy-ness." Glimpses of "holy-ness" tempt us to create patchworks of unsustainable complexity. We know what only we can know. Life sets us apart. Yet we can feel urgent needs to set other people in the exact same place where we have stood and share our elation. This is a dangerous impulse.

Sure, on indrawn breaths, this need to reach out has generated rhapsodies of art, of music, of performance and of liturgical and poetic expression. To hold onto the simplicity, and to reach that far from self-concern, most of us struggle to find concepts and voices that can bridge the boundaries between everyday language and our elusive, deepest, most extravagant experiences. The bridges are hard to find and we're merely human so, on exhalations, we've seen the same yearning to raise others sour into impulses to control. Anger, dogma, bullying and orthodoxy can be the outcomes. We can hope to be only as good as the "gods" we open to and, if horizons of greed and suspicion enclose our gods, they will be as vile as any that humanity's ever known.

Nevertheless, the fact that we can experience "god-ness" within is ample reason to make space in our lives and in our culture for explorations of holiness, of transcendence. The idea that mysteries are beyond our reach doesn't mean they don't exist. Our own existence is mysterious enough. And perplexity's a constant that underlies human awareness.

Certainty, and the hunger for it, is the danger. Certainties can always be shaken ... shaken, they turn to fear. Fear hangs on the edge of fury. Faith's the cure. Why? Because it's felt rather than asserted, faith gives us a relatively healthy place to play with the possibilities.

> *Beauty, like so much that touches us deeply, is an experience, not a statement. And, no. It is not "in the eye of the beholder." It exists independently, waiting to be discovered. It calls for attention and triggers feelings of intimate completion ... feelings of an immediate fit with even subconscious, and unexamined or unexpected yearnings. It can be at once soothing, energizing and disorienting. The moment might be ephemeral, but it can glow in our awareness of all things for the rest of our lives, challenging us to conform with its character. In this way, beauty draws us towards the fullness of our selves. I hold the view that beauty is god's language of love. And curiosity is the key to the mystery that opens "heaven" to us. "Heaven" happens when we open to mystery. It has to come, though, not as escape but as engagement. We are surrounded by beauty and mystery, every waking minute. We evolved to inhabit what we cannot know. We reject beauty and mystery when we assert that we "know" or "believe." "Heaven" is reality: fluid, dynamic, alive, a very real and concrete fantasy. It is a "fantasy" to the extent that it remains an aspiration; it is "real" and "concrete" in its power to change the world. And, when we damage what is beautiful in our attempts to turn material reality into*

"stuff," a casualty can be our capacity for love (the air that's breathed in Eden). Anyway, "stuff" is just damaged reality.

RELIGION'S no substitute for experience. At most, I've found it an optional complement to life—but one so life-enriching and emotionally expanding that I wouldn't want to puzzle my way through life without it. I'd waste far too much time. I find my "Christian" experience facilitates closeness, and brightens my awareness. It expands my appreciation of life, love and engagement.

Edward Slingerland, professor of Asian Studies at the University of British Columbia is, at the time this book is going to print, leading a team of more than 50 scientists, social scientists and humanities scholars from universities across North America, Europe and East Asia who are hoping to establish what religion is, how it is linked to morality, and why it plays such a ubiquitous role in human existence. They are midway through the $6 million, six-year project. "Despite its ubiquity and centrality to human affairs, religion remains, from an academic perspective, one of the least studied and most poorly understood aspects of human behaviour," the project's website states. A full report on the group's findings will be available in 2018, when the University of British Columbia plans to host a big public workshop and museum exhibition to illustrate its central findings.[78]

At least for the meantime, this gets me off the hook, except to note that human beings—all of us—have innate leanings towards curiosity and wonder.

It's not too odd to think about. Toolmaking's widely accepted as a species-wide trait, our genes inclining us to whittle a sharper spear, develop a faster, more prolific process, build a more powerful engine ... why shouldn't we be disposed to wondering about existence?

So let's think about engagement.

As I read it, what Jesus (for example) seemed to be on about was looking for harmonies with the moment and with others, with a bit of in-your-face critique for people who mess others up.

Morality, for him, seemed always to be about explorations of love's capacities: lifting others up. To some people that may sound a bit wimpy but it set him face-to-face against the Roman Empire and, despite its torturing and killing him, his way survived the Empire's collapse.

PERHAPS it's because love extends so far beyond the world of materiality while, at the same time, being so immediately, intimately and viscerally experienced, that it's easier to sing about love than to write about it.

But, it seems to me, it's vital to write about it, to talk about it, to think about it, express it, and live it. Love should be a public discourse: a hot political issue.

Love leaps and dances; it staves off every other emotion in its need to animate us. Love is the energy that makes goodness possible, appropriate and effective. I've seen it push aside good sense, need, fear and self-interest ... even sleep, food, sex and selfhood. It is love that makes hope not just possible, but irrepressible. And, while I've seen love make apparent "mistakes," it's always brought with it a gentleness of consequence.

Given its compelling, transforming power, and its essential goodness, it strikes me as odd that love's not more explicit in what we're allowed to see of "public life." Could love become an election issue? I think it should be THE election issue. If that sounds silly, here's a sidebar to the thought:

> *The power of placebos has puzzled physiologists for some time. It is a common, inescapably obvious phenomenon in drug trials. "Control group" members, given a sugar pill instead of the active drug being tested, often show a significant health enhancement by simply taking part. It works, even when people know they're getting a placebo rather than active treatment. It has also been found to work for animals. In 2015, Luana Colloca at the University of Maryland found placebo effects strengthened among women by vasopressin: a hormone that, among other things, heightens feelings of trust in women. A suggestion is that the attitude and manner of the person administering the placebo may also raise its effectiveness: "Social cues and interpersonal interactions strongly contribute to evoke placebo effects that are pervasive in medicine," she said.[79] Love, perhaps, could find a role in public health care.*

So, yes, love should be a political issue. It should saturate public affairs and international relations. What a joy it would be if, somewhere in the tides of government policy documents, there were expressions of unbridled, self-sacrificing love for other peoples … as, say, a diplomatic priority, or as the democratic necessity it is.

What goes around comes around. Imagine how liberating it would be to discover that our "enemies" loved us, despite our flaws and blindness … imagine our enemies covertly discovering that our priorities were focused on our love for them.

This may sound flippant. It's a "faith" idea, after all, so it should sound a bit crazy.

OF course, it would have to mean much more than the word "love" that pops up in the clichés, as a euphemism for sex or, most tritely and irrelevantly, as a synonym for "like." It has to be about other people because that's where love compels us to go. We love by throwing ourselves into love, not by gathering it in and holding onto it; love's dynamic, it's like a wind. Stilled, it ceases to exist. It's like that odd interface of matter and energy we call "life": it moves, it animates, it cannot be confined. And it is crucial that it be available to every person. To be secluded from love is to know greater cruelty than to be secluded from food or water.

How sad and dull is it to reduce "love" to stupid statements like "I'd love a cold beer," "I love my i-Pad," "I love that ad where they ..."—you mean you'd lay down your life and everything you have for the sake of that ad, i-Pad or beer? I don't think so.

Please, don't diminish the word by shriveling it to parity with its opposite: to "like" is to want for oneself; to "love" is to empty oneself into what is loved ... it had better be worthwhile.

Love's often ignited involuntarily out of affinity or attraction; it grows into a yearning to give your whole life over to the object of your love, as the need to push obstacles like ego and old hurts aside. This takes the discipline of deliberate will.

If love is not to die, then this clearing away of debris from the past—of fears, of irritations, of preconceptions, of angers, hurts and anxieties—has to be a delicious, liberating habit. It means embracing widening circles of love, simply because of the connections that link the living world and shape its dependence on the inanimate world.

When you know your lover needs to eat, you don't contaminate the food source. When you hear your lover's sleeping breath, you don't poison the air. When your lover drinks, do you foul the water or sour the wine? And, when your love has extended into the places of air and food, you'll yearn to reach beyond that. Your curiosity and all that's beautiful lead you on ... you'll see the fragility of all-important essence.

And nothing in life holds more value than experiences of that essence.

WHAT, then, is worthy of love? Well, we are ... you are, I am. And we should, I guess, be striving to make that clearer. How do we do that?

The best way is for our "selves" to drench "our selves" in outpourings of love. The more determinedly we do that, the easier it gets to love existence itself, and all that supports it: the blade of grass, the person in the passing car, remembered joys, the air, the sun, the planet ... the universe.

The universe? Really? Why not?

Our experience of the Universe has everything to do with its capacity to sustain us. If, out of love, we stand out of each other's sun and let it reach us, it's enormously generous ... and the more love we pour into the tiny part of it that we can reach, the better prepared we are to experience it.

In this way, we can move past "doing" some loving towards "becoming" a source of love.

A task that's taken on in the way of the Samoan canoe-builder—out of love for his son—has an array of outcomes, none of them predictable, from the weaving together of a number of related stories in which there is no single lead character. The outcomes are uncertain. They fall together into yet broader stories and themes that have directions rather than endings.

The person who's "becoming" can't wrest control from hostile or indifferent forces by matching them. Rather, the way ahead is to conform with places the brutes can't reach. Life can be one of those places when cycles of dance, play, struggle and survival mesh with the rhythmic certainties of sunrise and sunset, the succession of the seasons.

Eventually the brutes burn out. Their sources of energy are self-destructive. Fighting them headlong confirms them in their aggression and strengthens their power. The costs here are frightening because we long for safety and predictability and are appalled at the way so many of our stories seem to end. Moreover, we discover, certainty is an illusion.

We're called to more than "doing love." I think we're called to "BE" love. That's what I understand faith to be: the makings of a movement. It's the difference between going hunting, say, and becoming a hunter ... between a craft and an art.

> *Beauty re-contextualizes its contexts ... a single flower can re-color the sky, a bird's call can poise the whole world on the point of a pin, a flavor, or a fleeting aroma, can envelop a whole day, change a relationship or enchant an entire human memory. A beetle in the sun can break the grip of despair. A golden turn of words can transform bitter memories. The shape of a single leaf can smooth a crumpled soul. Beauty is god's language of love. Requiring oneself to seek, open and enter into experiences of beauty is the key to all of the "Edens" that surround us. We don't enter them ... they enter us.*

IT seems to have been "forever": a deep human need to find reassurance in mystery ... to find intimacy with existence.

"Reassurance" is relative. Across the board, though, can be found all sorts of happy similarities. The most daunting differences can be traced to short-lived cultural fashions, biases and practices, the imagined tastes of the "gods" having happily coincided with the culture's social sanctions. The similarities can more often be linked to widespread or universal human capacities, or to the daily needs of social animals: genes or survival.

No matter how the impulse is expressed, though, or where we find the shapes of its expression, the existential mysteries ever vex human consciousness. And the "god" hypothesis does not go away.

This is where atheism fails, not because of its apparently watertight rationality but because "god" does not go away. Whether or not "god" or the "gods" take form in the human mind or at the furthest ends of the universe, or exist all-pervasively, is irrelevant: we're just conjecturing out of our ignorance about the gods' location, not their existence. Whichever way, they are just as "present."

One way to escape the issue is to build a leaden wall around all that we think we know and name the wall "the ends of the universe": welcome to the modern, rational, practical man of action, the pragmatist who gets things done.

As a cultural style, it produces the literalist, the materialist, the rule of law, the authoritarian. Dualisms and fundamentalism thrive because you can only be "right" or "wrong." Minds close. All becomes egregious self-interest and unhappy vanity. And we make our most calamitous mistakes.

It doesn't expressly exclude "good" but the trap is that there's no "higher court" of appeal: there's no effective recourse for aesthetic, intuitive or "spiritual" values, and "emotionalism" is portrayed as a weakness. There's no Ma'at. Nothing is sacred.

We've moved a long way from the Middle Ages, when kings and "magic" pulled the strings, deep into the reign of the rational ... and the present danger's that we human beings have always tended to swing between extremes.

We need "religion", "spirituality" and "faith" to be fully human. And we're closest to "god" when we are closest to the wholeness of our own humanity... and to the whole of humanity.

This is the "bedrock" of faith ... not what's "believed" but where our foundations lie, in the fabric of our humanity. There's nothing as artless as "belief" about faith. It has to be about being. It's the context, not the content that's decisive. And the context is the absolute mystery of existence.

> *I used to believe it was me ...*
> *that I dreamt them up*
> *all on my own, but I don't:*
> *thoughts form themselves in me.*
> *Memories gather, lightly-linked,*
> *jostling like boys with a ball*
> *to tell their lies and tales and truths.*
> *The unforgotten, the odd,*
> *the unrehearsed, the new,*
> *even the wearied obsolete ...*
> *like oils, their perfumes merge:*
> *all the gathered tinctures,*
> *distillates of instants gone*
> *and long, loitering moments.*
> *Words, faces, places loved,*
> *musics of mood and emotion:*
> *countless iridescent flows.*
> *And they just form ...*
> *those fragments mingle,*
> *merge, elide, expand ...*
> *and then begin to breathe.*
> *Contradictions turn to paradox,*
> *rehearse harmonies and these*
> *then birth ideas of form, or fancy.*
> *Some gel, some rise, some glint*
> *some unspin as vortices,*
> *rippling in my blending bowl,*

> *then set like bedded rock.*
> *But always into shadow*
> *flits a form too fast to follow.*
> *This must be my soul: the jolly joiner*
> *of my past and present so tomorrow*
> *will seem real to me while, in fact,*
> *it's the imaginary me that's made*
> *strangely real to tomorrow.*

THERE are senses in which all roads point to some sort of "truth" in the end. Yet "the end" lies forever beyond our grasp. It's a set-up: a consequence of being sentient creatures with curiosity and memories. And of finding it impossible, even with super-computing, to reach beyond the context of our own species-specific consciousness.

But this is a state that needn't drop us into existential dismay. Rather, it teases us into taking the next step on a journey of mind, spirit and emotion towards a mystery we cannot fully penetrate. It makes life an adventure: a potentially fulfilling one.

> *A little bit of liking takes a little bit of trust. A little bit of trust calls for a little goodwill. And perhaps that's the seed, where it all begins, the one sustaining the other. "Friendship," we might call it. But, let's look inwards. I've fallen in love a few times, been rebuffed, then let it happen again. Love withheld is like a puppy in a cage, yapping and scratching to get out. Released, it can bound away to unforeseen distances. Given water and a hug of affection, the puppy will start trusting, not only the creature that shows it kindness but also, more importantly, its own impulse to become what it must. Met with kindness, we too tend to trust and love ... inwardly. The one emotion binds us to the other: love and faith blossom together. Betrayal, if it happens, lies outside of the love and faith that fuse together within. Faith's roots reach deeper than the noisy present. So does that inwardly-held living love. The semantic wall between "faith" and "love" becomes, like the distinction between inhaled and exhaled breaths, or one side of a balloon and the other, immaterial: it seldom matters.*

OUR cultures offer us ground plans for being. We know our existence is "real" because, although it baffles us, it seizes us and then, when we dare to trust it, we sense the vacuums that fear and needfulness leave behind.

"Truth" is such a vacuum: it draws us into itself. It excites our intellect and leads us to realizations of its limitations and fragility and, within that vulnerability, unbounded freedom. It excites all of our emotions then leaves them, like the friends of a departed traveller standing in the terminal as the aircraft lifts from the tarmac, to go reflectively home. The furthest we can reach is to awe and wonder. And that's not a bad place to be.

Trying to talk or, worse, write about it drops me into impasses of language, reason and imagination: it's like trying to chase one particular, stubborn sheep through the midst of a milling flock.

More and more as I explore, life's way seems studded with mystery's mementos. They're everywhere, tripping me into flashes of delight or sighs of yearning, sudden perplexity or apprehensions of beauty. At my fingertips, under my feet, lies an idea, a sound or a color: sunlight shining through pink, springtime lilac blossom perhaps, or the opening of a resting butterfly's wings, the song of a river over ancient rocks, the exhilaration of surf, and the heaving tranquility that's found beyond the breaker line. Time evaporates away and the moments take hold in some place beyond ordinary remembering.

THE beauty and variety of human cultures suggest to me that we layer thought onto experience, rather the way that a painter applies color to a canvas ... and that the act of seeing is what gives our surroundings their "reality" and demonstrates the essence of our creativity.

Do we expose ourselves to experience? Or do we impose ourselves on it?

> *Philosophers pall.*
> *Love's enough.*
> *Doglike, I doze in the sun:*
> *the wren trills her glee ...*

WE of the powerful West urgently need to find saner values if we're to put brakes on our powers of over-production and dispel the anaesthesia of self-inflating consumption and fleeting amusement.

I recently heard a film producer say that you couldn't make a commercially successful movie in which a child's pet is seen to die. He then went on to say that graphic depictions of violence, sex, conflagration and horror were box-office gold. Isn't there a disquieting conflict here between sentimentality and voyeurism? Then there are people like Jan Rezab—he describes himself as "an entrepreneur, founder, CEO and parent"—who contributed a column to *Forbes* in 2015 that described his acquiring the capacity to watch the fantasy saga *Game of Thrones* at twice the normal delivery speed: "speedwatching."[80] But, he wrote, "you can't just go from 1x speed to 2x speed. You have to take a natural progression. I started at 1.2x speed and built the speed up. As you continue to speed watch, higher speeds get easier and easier to comprehend. I've been speed watching for the last two years, and I now feel comfortable watching at 2x the normal viewing speed, with some types of videos, even faster." He found this helped him find more time for quality parenting.

Our economic systems disagree with us to the point that they make our souls wilt. Yet we seem able to sleep through the systemic violence that runs through our communities, relationships, language, social interactions and entertainment ... ostracism, for example, of the poor, patronisation of women and marginally disabled people, intolerance towards minorities, the stereotyping and victimisation of "other" ethnicities.

Too often, fear closes us to real-life social and cultural excitement beyond our immediate circles. Death and life, it often seems, both frighten us. Fears deter us from so much of what we might enjoy: in isolating us, they make us sad.

Again, I'm cornered: our most pressing need is for love. But it's not a silly hope.

> *WE can do it! One of the greatest gifts we have is the way we can slip from one way of thinking into another, almost seamlessly. We do it all the time. We can find each other in among the fogs of rush and noise. We can be delicately sensitive, even complicated, yet quickly cotton onto different conceptual worlds. We can understand, say, the logic of a board game one moment, switch to an online search the next, then turn and appreciate a piece of art. These easy accommodations put us at ease in our own homes and, in a very different way, in those of other people. They let us shift in a breath from doing a crossword to playing with a pet, or deepening the expression of our music-making. We can be immersed in the imaginary world of a novel and switch in a second to hear a blunt newscast about things we've never experienced in places we've never seen. Or relate to a neighbor's child. We can speak in many voices: hypothetically, emotionally, spiritually, demandingly, ironically, playfully, imaginatively, subtly, satirically, teasingly, threateningly or intellectually. We can engage with a political system, hold a job, cook a meal or tune a radio.*
>
> *This ability to flex and engage with so many ways of interacting and understanding is the foundation of friendship, and the shaping of a personality. It gives us our unique social presence. It equips us to live among others and arrive at understandings of society. It's this social versatility that makes us successful as a species. Moreover, it is to be vastly more cherished than rational "intelligence" or highly paid technical skills. This capacity is the linchpin of society. We can find friends and spend time with each other. Even where there's no shared language, we can sit down and, with little more than curiosity and respect, come to know and enjoy the company of strangers and people of very different cultures. We may*

have a lot to learn but we can do it.
We CAN know love. We CAN experience faith.
Anyway, what's "progress" worth without them?

A new morning? Maybe that's where it all begins?

References

[1] Rowan Hooper, "All hail the Anthropocene, the end of Holocene thinking," in *New Scientist,* no. 3013, 18 March 2015, p. 15.

[2] Nick Lane and William Martin, "The energetics of genome complexity" in *Nature,* vol. 467, issue 7318, pp. 929–934. Published online 20 October 2010 at: doi: 10.1038/nature09486. In this article's abstract, they write: "All complex life is composed of eukaryotic (nucleated) cells. The eukaryotic cell arose from prokaryotes just once in four billion years, and otherwise prokaryotes show no tendency to evolve greater complexity. Why not? Prokaryotic genome size is constrained by bioenergetics. The endosymbiosis that gave rise to mitochondria restructured the distribution of DNA in relation to bioenergetic membranes, permitting a remarkable 200,000-fold expansion in the number of genes expressed."

[3] "Kellogg launches hot cereal, bars, shakes and more for changing breakfast preferences," *PR Newswire* (New York), 6 June 2013. In the fourth quarter of 2014, incidentally, Kellogg posted a loss of $293 million compared to a profit of $1.1 billion the year before. The company's chief executive officer, John Bryant, said the reversal was "disappointing" and could be "mainly be attributed to continued poor performances in Special K and Kashi." Full-year net income in 2014 was $633 million, down 65 per cent from the previous year.

[4] See, for example, Nicole Meredith and Lorne Tepperman, *Outsights: Inequality from Inside and Out* (Rock's Mills Press, 2017).

[5] Bill McKibben, *The End of Nature* (New York: Random House, 1989), p. 58.

[6] Virgil, *Georgics: A New Translation by Peter Fallon* (Oxford University Press, 2006), Book 3, lines 284–287, p.60.

[7] A 2003 New Zealand study, for example, examined these issues. See: Susan G. Singley and Paul Callister, "Work poor or working poor? A comparative perspective on New Zealand's jobless households" (*Social Policy Journal of New Zealand,* issue 20, June 2003), pp. 134–155: "Overall the literature would suggest that while there is a range of potential benefits from being in paid work for both individuals and households, for many households, a shift from being work poor to becoming part of the working poor provides few gains in wellbeing. Gains in economic wellbeing and child outcomes seem to be stronger when the incomes of the working poor are boosted with income transfers. Thus, any policies developed to address New Zealand's relatively high levels of work poverty, particularly among child-rearing households, need to be formulated in ways that prevent the growth of working poverty."

[8] Nicole Gombay, "Today is today and tomorrow is tomorrow: Reflections on Inuit understanding of time and place" in B. Collignon and M. Therrien (eds.), *Orality in the 21st Century: Inuit Discourse and Practices (Proceedings of the 15th Inuit Studies Conference), Paris, 2006* (INALCO, 2009). Published online at: http://www.inuitoralityconference.com.

[9] Amanda Gefter, "About time: Countdown to the theory of everything," *New Scientist,* no. 2833, 11 October 2011, p. 41–42.

[10] Tim Rice, *May It Fill Your Soul: Experiencing Bulgarian Music* (University of Chicago Press, 1994).

[11] In her column on page 2 of the *Toronto Star* on 17 February 2016, Rosie DiManno noted that at least 66 countries were then engaged in wars. These wars

involved 686 armies, militias, terrorist organizations, guerrilla groups and separatist movements.

[12] See: A.H. Clough (ed.), *Plutarch's Lives: The Dryden Translation* (Bantam, 2007).

[13] Era Dabla-Norris, Kalpana Kochhar, Frantisek Ricka, Nujin Suphaphiphat, and Evridiki Tsounta (with contributions from Preya Sharma and Veronique Salins), *Causes and Consequences of Income Inequality: A Global Perspective* (Strategy, Policy, and Review Department, International Monetary Fund, June 2015).

[14] John Maynard Keynes. *Essays in Persuasion* (New York: W.W. Norton & Co., 1963), p. 358–373.

[15] Bruno Latour, *The Effects of Capitalism,* accessed 6 August 2014 at https://www.youtube.com/watch?v=8i-ZKfShovs. A draft of his presentation can be accessed at http://www.bruno-latour.fr/sites/default/files/136-AFFECTS-OF-K-COPENHAGUE.pdf.

[16] See: Peter Adamson, "Child well-being in rich countries: A comparative overview," UNICEF *Innocenti Report Card 11* (Florence, 2011) at http://www.unicef-irc.org/publications/pdf/rc11_eng.pdf), p. 3.

[17] Harry J. Holzer, Diane Whitmore Schanzenbach, Greg J. Duncanc and Jens Ludwig, "The economic costs of childhood poverty in the United States" (*Journal of Children and Poverty* 14: 1, March 2008*)*.

[18] See, for example: World Food and Agriculture Organization, *Statistical Yearbook, Section 3, 2012*. Accessed at: http://www.fao.org/docrep/015/i2490e/i2490e03a.pdf, 2 April 2015.

[19] Ross McDonald. *Money Makes You Crazy: Custom and Change in the Solomon Islands* (Dunedin, New Zealand: University of Otago Press, 2003), pp. 11–12.

[20] See: Samantha Nutt, *Damned Nations: Greed, Guns, Armies and Aid* (McClelland & Stewart, 2011).

[21] World Bank, Office of the Chief Economist for the Africa Region, *Africa's Pulse: An Analysis of Issues Shaping Africa's Economic Future* (Vol. 11, April 2015). http://www.worldbank.org/content/dam/Worldbank/document/Africa/Report/Africas-Pulse-brochure_Vol11.pdf.

[22] For details of sealing and whaling in the Chatham Islands, see: Rhys Richards, *Whaling and Sealing in the Chatham Islands* (Canberra: Roebuck, 1982).

[23] W. Herbert Guthrie-Smith, *Sorrows and Joys of a New Zealand Natura*list (Dunedin: Reed, 1936), p. 218

[24] G. W. Gesner, "Dr. Abraham Gesner: A Biographical Sketch" (*Bulletin No. XIV*, Natural History Society of New Brunswick, 1896).

[25] See, for example: H.P. Lee, P.K. Chae, H.S. Lee, and Y.K. Kim, in *Psychiatry Research*, 150:1, pp. 21–32 (e-published 31 January, 2007 at: http://www.ncbi.nlm.nih.gov/pubmed/17270278).

[26] Information accessed 15 October 2015, at: http://www.lotterycanada.com/lotto-max and linked pages.

[27] James Surowieki, "Open Season" in *The New Yorker*, 21 October 2013, p. 31.

[28] See: Elizabeth Barlow, "The New York Magazine Environmental Teach-In" in *New York Magazine,* 30 March 1970.

[29] See: James Knowles, "Jonson's entertainment at Britain's burse" in Martin Butler (ed.), *Re-Presenting Ben Jonson: Text, History, Performance* (Palgrave Macmillan, 1999), pp. 159–180.

[30] Stephen Hawking, Stuart Russell, Max Tegmark, Frank Wilczek, "Stephen Hawking: *Transcendence* looks at the implications of artificial intelligence—but are we taking AI seriously enough?" in *The Independent,* 1 May 2014.

31 Jan Zalasiewicz, Mark Williams, Will Steffan and Paul Crutzen, "The new world of the Anthropocene (synopsis)" in *Environmental Science and Technology,* 44: 7 (American Chemical Society, 2010), p. 2228.
32 The American Academy of Anti-Aging Medicine, "Join the anti-aging marketplace" (exhibitor information) at: http://www.a4m.com/conferences-exhibitors-anti-aging-marketplace.html.
33 Albert Einstein, "The world as I see it," *Living Philosophies,* vol. 84, *Forum* magazine series (Simon & Schuster, 1930), p. 194. Published online in an abridged form at http://www.aip.org/history/einstein/essay.htm.
34 See: R. Belk, "Abstract," *Possessions and Self* (Wiley, 1988).
35 See: Robert A. Paul, *Mixed Messages: Cultural and Genetic Inheritance in the Constitution of Human Society* (University of Chicago Press, 2015).
36 Brigid Schulte, *Overwhelmed: Work, Love, and Play When No One Has the Time* (Farrar, Straus and Giroux, 2014).
37 Liz Else, "Resistance is not futile" (*New Scientist,* no. 2988, 30 September 2014), pp. 28–30.
38 See: Anthony Storr, *Solitude: A Return to the Self* (Flamingo, 1988).
39 See: Thomas Merton, *Thoughts in Solitude* (1956), published in various editions.
40 William Deresiewicz, "The end of solitude," *Chronicle of Higher Education,* 30 January 2009.
41 Timothy D. Wilson, David A. Reinhard, Erin C. Westgate, Daniel T. Gilbert, Nicole Ellerbeck, Cheryl Hahn, Casey L. Brown and Adi Shaked (2014), "Just think: The challenges of the disengaged mind" (*Science* 4, vol. 345, no. 6192), pp. 75–77.
42 Miguel Farias and Catherine Wikholm, "Ommm ... aargh!" in *New Scientist* (226: 3021, 16 May 2015), pp. 28–29.
43 James Holland, *Heroes: The Greatest Generation and the Second World War* (Harper Perennial, 2006), p. 323.
44 E. B. "Scotch" Paterson, *Cassino to Trieste: A Soldier's Story* (Steele Roberts, New Zealand, 2004), p. 166.
45 Frederick S. Perls, *Gestalt Therapy Verbatim* (Bantam Books, fifth edition, 1972; originally published in English by Real People Press, 1969).
46 British Geological Survey, *Climate Change: Landscape Impact* (published online at http://www.bgs.ac.uk/anthropocene/LandscapeImpact.html).
47 See: Tepilit Ole Saitoti, *The Worlds of a Maasai Warrior: An Autobiography* (University of California Press, 1988), p. 117.
48 See, for example: Michel Foucault, trans. Richard Howard, *Madness and Civilization: A History of Insanity in the Age of Reason* (Vintage/Random House, New York, 1988).
49 Magnus Linklater, "Arctic explorer is finally forgiven for telling truth" in *The Times* (London), 27 September 2014, p. 13. And: Ken McGoogan, *Fatal Passage: The Untold Story of John Rae, the Arctic Adventurer Who Discovered the Fate of Franklin* (Harper Collins, 2002).
50 See: Duane Roller (trans.), *The Geography of Strabo: An English Translation, with Introduction and Notes* (Cambridge University Press, 2014).
51 See, for example: Peter Levi (trans.): *Pausanais' Guide to Greece, Vol. 1: Central Greece* and *Guide to Greece, Vol. 2: Southern Greece* (Penguin Classics, 1984).
52 *Frontiers of Human Neuroscience,* 27 May 2014, at http://dx.doi.org/10.3389/fnhum.2014.00203.
53 See, for example: Carol Zaleski, *Otherworld Journeys: Accounts of Near-Death Experience in Medieval and Modern Times* (Oxford University Press, 1987).

54 Viktor Frankl, *The Unheard Cry for Meaning* (Simon & Schuster, 1978), p. 72.
55 Roderick Frazier Nash, "Power of the wild" in *New Scientist*, No. 2336, 30 March 2002, pp. 42–44.
56 See: Roderick Frazier Nash, *The Rights of Nature: A History of Environmental Ethics* (University of Wisconsin Press, 1989).
57 See: E.O. Wilson, *Half Earth: Our Planet's Fight for Life* (Liveright, 2016), and *The Social Conquest of Earth* (Liveright, 2013).
58 See John 18:38.
59 See, for example: Charles C. Man, "The birth of religion" in *National Geographic* (June 2011), pp. 35–59. Or: Elif Btuman, "The sanctuary: The world's oldest temple and the dawn of civilization," *The New Yorker*, 19 December 2011.
60 See: Robert Price, *The Pre-Nicene New Testament: Fifty-four Formative Texts* (Signature Books, 2006).
61 See, for example: *Medieval Sourcebook: The Golden Legend (Aurea Legenda)*. Compiled by Jacobus de Voragine, 1275, "Englished" by William Caxton, 1483. Available online at: http://www.aug.edu/augusta /iconography/goldenLegend.
62 Richard Sharp (trans.), *Life of Saint Columba* (Penguin Classics, 1995). Available online at: http://www.fordham.edu/halsall/basis/columba-e.asp.
63 See: Website of the Temple of the Jedi Order at http://www.templeof thejediorder.org. Also: Debra McCormick, "From Jesus Christ to Jedi knight: Changing paradigms in the study of religious affiliation," TASA conference, University of Western Australia and Murdoch University, 4–7 December 2006). Available online at: http://www.tasa.org.au/conferences/conferencepapers06/papers/Open/McCormick.pdf.
64 Michael D. Coogan, ed., *The New Oxford Annotated Bible: New Revised Standard Version* (Oxford University Press, 2011), Acts 9: 3–9 (pp. 1936–1937).
65 *Ibid.*, Zechariah 9: 9–10 (p. 1345).
66 *Ibid.*, John 13: 34–35 (pp. 1936–1937).
67 See, for example: Te Rangi Hiroa (Sir Peter Buck), *Vikings of the Sunrise* (J.B. Lippincott, Philadelphia, 1938); and *The Coming of the Maori* (R.W. Stiles, 1925; Whitcombe and Tombs, 1949).
68 D. Kopenawa and B. Albert, *The Falling Sky: Words of a Yanomami Shaman* (Bellknap/Harvard University Press, 2013).
69 Coogan, *New Oxford Annotated Bible,* Matthew 6:19–21 (p. 1755).
70 Elaine Pagels, *Revelations: Visions, Prophesy, and Politics in the 'Book of Revelation'* (Viking, 2012), pp. 92–93.
71 See: Coogan, *New Oxford Annotated Bible,* John 8: 58 (p. 1898).
72 See: *Ibid.*, Matthew 8: 20 (p. 1758): "Jesus replied, 'Foxes have holes and birds of the air have nests; but the Son of Man has nowhere to lay his head.' "
73 The Chinese Text Project has made some of Mozi's writings available in translation online at: http://ctext.org/mozi (accessed 7 October 2014).
74 See: Coogan, *New Oxford Annotated Bible,* Mark 2:27
75 *Ibid.*, Matthew 12:46–50 (p. 1765).
76 See: Herodotus, *On The Customs of the Persians, c. 430 BCE*. Available online at: http://www.fordham. edu/Halsall/ancient/herodotus-persians.asp.
77 Cited variously, including: Smith, Wilfred Cantwell, *The Meaning and End of Religion* (Fortress Press, 1963), p. 30.
78 Cultural Evolution of Religion Research Consortium. "Central research questions: Are religious beliefs and behaviors linked to within-group solidarity and cooperation?" Centre for Human Evolution, Cognition, and Culture,